Wisdom of
Numerology

Suzan Owens

LUMINOUS MOON PRESS
BOULDER, COLORADO

Published by Luminous Moon Press, LLC, Boulder, CO

Cover and interior layout and design by Carolyn Oakley,
Luminous Moon Design + Press | luminousmoon.com

First Edition
First Printing: December 2022

Publication Data
Suzan Owens
Wisdom of Numerology

ISBN-13: 979-8-9874864-0-5

BODY, MIND & SPIRIT / Numerology — BODY, MIND & SPIRIT /
Inspiration & Personal Growth

Printed and bound in the United States of America

For Andrea and Roslyn

Contents

Introduction

Metaphysics is a lifetime passion for me. I discovered Numerology in the early 90's and I was fascinated. Numerology came easy to me and made sense. I am not a mathematician, nor have I ever enjoyed math, but Numerology is different. Numbers are simply added, subtracted, and reduced to a single digit. I apply the principles of Numerology to bring a greater understanding of my gifts and talents, who I am, and my purpose in life.

When I was 21 years old, I nearly died in a car wreck. When I was 29, my mother passed away and 20 years later, my father passed. Each time I had the same number transiting my chart. I know when that number appears, it brings great change and powerful life lessons. Through Numerology, I see when life is a challenge, and the times of potential growth.

Numerology changed my life. I have an understanding of numbers and how they influence my life. Since I have been working with numbers, my life has made more sense and has a flow that I understand. Numerology is the structure, the paradigm in which I navigate my life.

I continually study many charts, including my own, to fully comprehend the number vibrations. Our numbers are specific to us, however we choose the energy we wish to express. When we are harmonious, our lives are fulfilled, balanced and productive. If we choose passive focus, we float through life, missing opportunities. Choosing the negative side allows for destruction and chaos. When I am clear about the energy of the number and how the different vibrations affect my life, I make decisions in regards to the vibrational energy.

Numerology runs in a nine year cycle. Having an understanding of each year's numerical energy, I know how to live in harmony with that vibration to create a more balanced and productive year. To calculate the year, add all the digits of the year together. For instance, 2023 is a seven year: $2 + 2 + 3 = 7$. On the following page is a quick definition of each year's number.

1 **A one year** is focused outward as you plant seeds for what you want to accomplish in the next nine years.

2 A **two year** is an inward focus, for you nurture your seeds and is slower than the previous year.

3 A **three year** is a blending of the previous years and a time when creativity flows. It is a social year, fast-paced, and outwardly focused time.

4 A **four year** is a year to set up a new foundation with your nose to the grindstone. You'll work hard this year and create a structure stable enough to see you through the changing five year.

5 The outwardly focused **five year** is all about freedom and expansion. This is your year to grow and you'll need the grounding of the four year for stability during this highly volatile time.

6 The **six year** is home and family and a time to integrate all the previous five years. Relationships and responsibility are the focus in this inward year.

7 The spiritual **seven year** is a time for inner reflection and self improvement. Ask life's big questions and do your research. Go on a vision quest.

8 The **eight year** is a time to direct your management and organizational skills toward self mastery. This is an outward year when money flows in greater frequency.

9 The inner reflective **nine year** is about endings and rebirths. Let go of what is no longer needed to make space for the new seeds to plant next year.

I have spent thousands of hours studying charts and doing readings for clients. Each chart I read presents a new interpretation of life and an opportunity to see yourself differently. Numerology presents a new perspective in which to view yourself, but also an understanding of your talents and why you have certain behaviors. It gives you a picture of your past and present as well as possibilities for your future. In writing this book, I am bringing those thousands of hours of study to you so that you, too, can benefit from the power of this practice.

I wrote *Wisdom of Numerology* to generate more interest in the science of Numerology. The compact, easy-to-read format of this book gives you the necessary information to have a basic understanding of Numerology. My book is an informational guide to each number and created for quick reference. This is a simple, but comprehensive guide for beginners who want to understand the numbers and their energy. It includes easy calculations to create your own beginning chart. In the back of the book is a worksheet for more advanced calculations to complete a comprehensive chart as well. As you grow in your practice with Numerology your use of this book grows with you.

The first section of this book includes introductory material oriented in the practice of Numerology. It contains definitions of common terms and a good general introduction to the practice of Numerology.

The main section is information about each number, including master numbers. Each number is clearly defined along with their different influences depending on where they appear on your chart. Use this section as a reference or read through it to get the full sweep of the progression through the numbers.

Finally, the back of the book has all the information needed to calculate a chart, which may be ordered through my website, www.wisdomofnumerology.com.

As an introductory explanation, use your birthday to understand your life path, your gifts, some potential high points and challenges in your life.

The birth date of this book is January 3, 2022. I chose this day to begin writing my book because this date calculates to a one day, which is a day for new beginnings and planting seeds for the future. The number one energy is creatively original, ambitious and successful. Having this birthday gives this book an independent and entrepreneurial vibration which allows it to stand alone.

My hope is this book generates interest in Numerology and you learn what numbers can teach you about your gifts and talents; about your soul's desire and how you present yourself to others. I want you to understand how important your birthday is and the effect number vibrations have as they flow through your life. My intention with this book is to present you with an understanding of Numerology that gives you the tools and ability to navigate your universe.

SECTION 1

A Quick Guide to Numerology

Numerology Grid

Numerology analyzes the inner/spiritual realms and the outer/physical world. If applied to our birth name and birthday, the number energy has a profound influence on our lives. Studying Numerology gives us the ability to see our gifts, talents as well as our challenges and lessons in life. When we know what numbers influence our personal chart, we can see our strengths and work in harmony with them. We are also able to see when challenges may arise and how to learn the most from missing numbers. When we know which number vibration is at its peak, we can work in harmony with the number vibration to achieve the greatest result.

Every letter has a numerical value associated with it, based on its position in the alphabet.

A is the first letter, (1)

J is the 10th letter, (10)

S is the 19th letter, (19)

When reduced to a single digit, (19) becomes $1 + 9 = 10$, $1 + 0 = 1$.

19 and 10 both reduce to number 1. So, A, J, and S all have the same numerical value, 1.

Reducing numbers is the key to Numerology.

Reducing numbers is the key to Numerology.

Below is the alphabet/number grid and is the foundation of Numerology. The letters and attached values never change regardless of where they appear on a chart. Pythagoras developed this chart to use when calculating your Core Numbers, Essence, and Transit Cycles.

1 = A, J, S
2 = B, K, T
3 = C, L, U
4 = D, M, V
5 = E, N, W
6 = F, O, X
7 = G, P, Y
8 = H, Q, Z
9 = I, R

Quick Number Reference

NUMBER 1. *Leader, Inventor, Entrepreneur, Achiever, CEO*

One individuals must stand on their own. Be assertive, not aggressive; ambitious and self-sufficient, not arrogant and domineering. Be courageous and innovative. Establish your individuality and independence. One energy is masculine; focused, rational; can be stubborn, willful and impulsive. Dislikes being overlooked.

AJS – 1

A (1): Leader, Independent, Ambitious, Self-Centered, Opinionated, Driven, Stubborn

J (10): Good Memory, Sincere, Ethical, Loyal, Procrastinates, Sincere, Clever

S (19): Achiever, Creative, Individualist, Spiritual, Impulsive, Charismatic, Passionate

NUMBER 2. *Diplomat, Moderator, Peacekeeper, Counselor, Artist, Healer, Sensitive*

Two individuals are excellent partners. Be supportive, understanding and tactful, not critical and co-dependent.

Two energy is feminine, receptive, intuitive, captivating and detail oriented; can be self conscious, overly sensitive and meddlesome. Follow your intuition, set boundaries and strive for balance. Establish reciprocal relationships and security.

BKT – 2

B (2): Emotional, Sensitive, Loyal, Shy, Introspective, Seeks Harmony, Critical

K (11): Intuitive, Emotional, Detail Oriented, Promotes Peace, Avoids Conflict. Nervous, Difficulty Letting Go

T (20): Diplomacy, Intuition, Cooperation, Protective, Over-emotional, Dynamic

NUMBER 3. *Artist, Musician, Speaker, Teacher, Salesperson, Visionary, Entertaining, Spontaneous*

Three is the unification of the originating one energy with the germinating two energy: the synthesis of creation. Three individuals are uplifting, optimistic, and artistic.

Be creative, spontaneous and versatile, not lazy, unfocused and scattered. Three energy is enthusiastic, imaginative and adaptable; can be overly dramatic, unfocused and critical. Loves life's adventures; dislikes routine and the mundane. Establish a joyful, creative lifestyle with discipline as the foundation.

CLU – 3

C (3): Creativity, Inspiring, Social, Demonstrative, Optimistic, Expressive, Scattered

L (12): Driving Force, Intellectual, Sincere, Travel, Inner Peace, Requires Balance, Self-Improvement

U (21): Universal Brotherhood, Peace, Universal Wisdom, Intuitive, Intelligent, Emotional, Indecisive, Sensuous, Fame

NUMBER 4. *Business Manager, Lawyer, Accountant, Administrator, Builder, Scientist, Worker-bee*

Four individuals are goal oriented, diligent and focused on achievement. Determined, productive and effective, not rigid, overly cautious and stubborn. Be focused and organized, not rigid and unyielding. Lighten up sometimes and look outside the box. Four energy is organized, dedicated and dependable; can be argumentative, repressed and tedious. Four vibration is determined, practical and excels at achieving objectives. Best number for mundane tasks. Dislikes unexpected change, poverty and loss. Scientist.

DMV – 4

D (4): Successful when in alliance with positive energy and living responsibly. Practical, Shrewd, Stubborn, Health Issues

M (13): Mentally focused, Diligent, Energetic, Efficient, Endurance, Impatient

V (22): Diligent, Insightful, Planner, Sincere, Loyal, Eccentric, Possessive, Opinionated

NUMBER 5. *Adventurer, Promoter, Actor, Public Figure, Salesperson*

Five individuals are freedom seekers and desire to live life to the fullest. Be adaptable, accept diversity and variety, but don't quit too early or change for the sake of change. Five is rapid energy for expansive growth, but can be unpredictable and unsettling. Stay centered, grounded and disciplined. Fives like adventure, competition and the unconventional, but dislike routine and the mundane. Five vibration is sensual, charismatic and influential but is prone to procrastination and addiction.

ENW – 5

E (5): Adventurous, Freedom Seeker, Passionate, Social, Expressive, Adaptable, Scattered, Impulsive, Undisciplined

N (14): Intuitive, Creative, Unconventional, Sensual, Versatile, Jealous, Overindulgent

W (23): Determined, Charismatic, Purposeful, Stimulating, Articulate, Unstable, Selfish, Procrastinates, Greedy

NUMBER 6. *Caregiver, Service Oriented, Responsible, Counselor, Healer*

Six individuals are stable and nurturing homebodies who desire to be of service. Be stable, conventional and settled, but not codependent and a martyr. Desires to create a safe, harmonious environment and loves to nurture family. Dislikes instability, insecurity and unfamiliarity. Establish healthy harmonious relationships both at home and career. Balance others' needs with your own; don't overdo.

FOX – 6

F (6): Responsible, Domestic, Compassionate, Empathic, Self-Sacrificing, Codependent, Depressed.

O (15): Strong Willed, Perseverance, Conservative, Patient, Respectful, Jealous, Virtuous or Corrupt

X (24): Perceptive, Sensual, Artistic, Charismatic, Higher realms into physical plane, Humanitarian, Crossroads in Consciousness, Nervous, Temperamental

NUMBER 7. *Seeker, Researcher, Spiritualist, Analyst, Philosopher, Consultant, Computer Analyst*

Seven individuals are truth seekers and search for the meaning of life and a spiritual path.

Be private and philosophical but not reclusive and critical. Be analytical and meditative, but not unapproachable, pessimistic and cynical. Desires deep spiritual connection and requires solitude for inner reflection. Dislikes the limelight, social interactions and demanding relationships. The most metaphysical of the numbers. Find time to meditate in nature.

GPY – 7

G (7): Intellectual, Introspective, Methodical Research, Meditation, Metaphysics, Psychic, Disciplined, Impulsive

P (16): Intelligent, Expressive, Reflection, Aloof, Dominating Possessive, Impatient

Y (25): Freedom Seeker, Psychic, Perceptive, Courageous, Ambitious, Secretive, Indecisive

NUMBER 8. *Business Owner/Manager, Executive, Entrepreneur, Engineer, Financier, Judge, Publisher*

Eight individuals are achievement oriented managers and excellent decision makers. Dislikes less capable superiors and being at the mercy of circumstances. Prefers to be the authority and in control of the environment to achieve power and status. Be decisive and delegate, but don't micromanage and manipulate. Be focused, organized and ambitious but not aggressive, judgmental and shrewd. Don't micromanage.

HQZ – 8

H (8): Original, Creative, Successful, Business Mind, Money, Authority, Power, Greedy, Selfish

Q (17): Successful, Leader, Authority, Intelligent, Original, Influential, Boring, Verbose

Z (26): Spiritual, Optimistic, Dynamic, Ambitious, Diplomacy, Intuitive, Stubborn, Impulsive, Impatient

NUMBER 9. *Humanitarian, Minister, Spiritualist, Psychic, Community Leader, Bodyworker, Artist, Actor*

Nine individuals are dreamers in search of Universal Harmony and the betterment of humankind.

Be idealistic, understanding, forgiving and tolerant but not aimless and gullible. Dislikes restrictions and out of control emotions. Seeks to make a global impact and raise the level of mass consciousness. Follows the Golden Rule and is benevolent, compassionate and creative, but can lose focus.

IR – 9

I (9): Emotional, Considerate, Creative, Intuitive, Compassionate, Spiritually Guided, Nervous, Temperamental

R (18): Gentle, Kind, Natural Leader, Uplift Humanity, Overly emotional, Memory challenges, Critical, Intolerant

LIFE CYCLES

0-9 yrs	Nursery, Intellect and Learning
9-18	Teenage, Sensitivity and Emotion
18-27	Bachelor, Enthusiasm and Drive
27-36	Nesting, Career and the Material
36-45	Adulthood, Inspiration and Change
45-54	Spiritual, Spirituality and Money
54-63	Relationship, Home and Family
63-72	Achievement, Completion and the Practical
72+	Wisdom, Unashamed Self Expression

Master Numbers

MASTER NUMBER 11/2. *Inventor, Counselor, Minister, Celebrity, Spiritualist, Writer, Spiritual, Teacher*

Eleven carries the same energy as the two, but with a higher spiritual vibration with the double one. This is a gift from the Universe and carries a responsibility to follow this master number path. You have the ability to raise the consciousness of humanity with a master number. You have free will, however and may choose not to live with this higher vibration. You will revert to the energy of the two. Refer to the number two for more information. Operating with the master number is always a choice.

Eleven individuals are intuitive messengers whose purpose is to inspire humanity with their spiritual truths. Eleven energy is highly intuitive, transformative and philosophical, but can easily be overstimulated and overly sensitive. Dislikes limitations and anything unpleasant or visually distressing. Enlightenment is the objective of the Eleven and then to become a spiritual teacher. Master number eleven is higher consciousness energy integrated with the number two.

MASTER NUMBER 22/4. *Global Entrepreneur, World Leader, Public Development, Master Builder, Producer, CEO*

Twenty-two carries the same energy as the four, but with a higher spiritual vibration of the double two. This is a gift from the Universe and carries a responsibility to follow this master number path. You have the ability to leave a legacy that can uplift humanity with a master number. You have free will, however and may choose not to live with this higher vibration. You will revert to the energy of the four. Refer to number four for more information. Operating with the master number is always a choice.

Twenty-two individuals unite higher consciousness with practical missions to build a legacy. Twenty-two energy is committed, tenacious, enthusiastic and able to see the big picture, but can be a workaholic and take on too much. Usually a forward thinker and ahead of their time, twenty-twos can be misunderstood and underappreciated. Master number twenty-two is higher consciousness energy integrated with the number four.

MASTER NUMBER 33/6. *World Leader, Global Human Services, Skilled Master Healer, Universal Earth Mother*

Thirty-three carries the same energy as the six, but with a higher spiritual vibration of the double three. This is a gift from the Universe and carries a responsibility to follow this master number path. You have the ability to raise the consciousness of humanity with a master number. You have free will, however and may choose not to live with this higher vibration. You will revert to the energy of the six. Refer to the number six for more information. Operating with the master number is always a choice.

Thirty-three individuals are compassionate, unconditionally loving and concerned with humanity on a global scale, but may be challenged to surrender personal ambitions. Thirty-three energy is Christ-like, healing, unconditionally loving, spiritual and altruistic. The mission is to bring spiritual truths to the material world and to heal and elevate mass consciousness. Always work for the greater good and betterment of humanity. If selfish concerns take precedence, challenges arise.

Quick Definition Reference

BIRTHDAY

Your day of birth (excluding the month and year) defines the gifts you brought with you in this lifetime. It reveals your many talents and career directions.

CHALLENGE NUMBER

The four challenge numbers are derived from the birthday and are on the same timeline as pinnacle numbers (see below for pinnacle definition). Challenges are obstacles to be overcome; lessons to be learned for you to reach your full potential. When you courageously face the challenge and learn the lesson, you are able to reach the full potential of the pinnacle.

CORE NUMBERS

These are the five core numbers in a chart: Life Path, Destiny, Soul, Personality, Maturity. The numbers are derived from your birthdate and the name on your birth certificate. They do not change in a lifetime.

CURRENT NAME NUMBER

This is your signature and the name you are called. This number can change throughout a lifetime and brings in different number energy every time you change your name. Changing a current name alters your chart by adding or deleting different number vibrations. It does not change your original core numbers, it only adds to them.

DESTINY NUMBER

The name on your birth certificate defines areas where you have the most potential for success in your life. The destiny number is your mission in life and guides you towards developing areas in your life to reach your full potential. This is your inner life goal.

ESSENCE NUMBER

The essence number is derived from the letters in your name and how they appear on your transit chart. The cycle runs from birthday to birthday, but the same number may repeat for many years unlike the personal year number.

KARMIC DEBT NUMBERS

Karmic debt numbers appear as 13/4, 14/5, 16/7, 19/1 and signify a past lifetime of abuse. These are now lessons to be mastered in this lifetime. They are most influential when they appear in the core numbers: Life Path, Destiny, Soul, Personality, Maturity, or Birthdate.

LIFE PATH
The life path number is derived from your birthdate and remains a constant influence throughout your life. It represents your talents and abilities received at birth which you will use to achieve your destiny. It reveals challenges to be mastered in this lifetime and special lessons to be learned. It is the most influential number in your core numbers.

MAJOR CYCLE
There are three major cycles in a lifetime and these are derived from your birthday. The first is the formative cycle and is ruled by the month of your birth. The second, or progressive cycle, is derived from the day of your birth. The third is called your wisdom cycle and is calculated from your birth year. The pinnacles and challenges are calculated from these three birthday numbers. The major cycles act as an umbrella over the pinnacles and challenges.

MASTER NUMBERS
11, 22, and 33 are master numbers. They could be reduced by adding the two numbers but as double digits you also read them as master numbers. They represent a higher vibration of the reduced number: 11/2, 22/4, 33/6. They carry a spiritual influence and indicate a time of greater understanding of a higher level of consciousness. This is a wondrous spiritual gift and if ignored, the energy reduces to the lower, reduced number.

MATURITY NUMBER
The life path number and destiny number combined create the maturity number. This influential core number reveals your future potential and ultimate goal of life. It is activated later in life and is useful when focused on possible career choices.

MISSING NUMBER
These are numbers which do not appear in your name and indicate a lesson to be learned in this lifetime; an underdeveloped trait or area out of balance. The intensity is lessened if the number is also a core number. If the missing number appears as a challenge number, the energy is heightened. Missing numbers are opportunities to learn which cannot be avoided. Lessons appear throughout a lifetime.

MULTIPLE NUMBERS
A number which is repeated many times in your name represents a proficiency or your area of expertise. These numbers represent a specific strength or ability. They are your strong points, which may be carried to extremes. Too many of a particular number is too much of a good thing and represents lessons that need to be learned.

PERSONAL YEAR
Numerology functions on a nine-year cycle and your personal year changes every January. It is calculated from adding your birth month and birth day with the current year.

1: New Beginnings, Action
2: Cooperation, Balance
3: Communication, Expression

4:     Building, Planning
5:     Movement, Change
6:     Responsibility, Universal Love
7:     Introspection, Personal Growth
8:     Karmic Justice, Power
9:     Endings, Completions
11/2: Illumination, Higher Learning
22/4: Accomplishment, Transformation
33/6: Universal Healer, Nurturer

PERSONALITY NUMBER

The personality number is derived from the consonants in your name. It is the "outer you" and the person you project to the world. The number you are seen as if you were to be described by someone else. This is not necessarily your true self and hence is a lesser influential number in the chart.

PINNACLE NUMBER

There are four pinnacles in a lifetime and they are derived from your birthday. The four pinnacle numbers are derived from the birthday and are on the same timeline as challenge numbers (see above for challenge definition). These four phases of life indicate the conditions and opportunities present in each pinnacle.

PLANES OF EXPRESSION

These numbers represent how you express yourself in the world physically, mentally, emotionally or intuitively. These numbers describe your behavior, thoughts, feelings and how you intuit.

SOUL NUMBER

The soul number is derived from the vowels in your name and reveals your true heart's desire. This is the "inner you" number and reveals your passions in life. Following this number feeds your soul.

TABLE OF EVENTS

All numbers transiting your chart throughout your lifetime: Essence, Personal Year, Major Cycle, Pinnacle and Challenges.

TRANSIT CHART

These are all the numbers that move through your Numerology Chart: Essence, Personal Year, Major Cycles, Pinnacles, and Challenges.

SECTION 2

Detailed
Number Descriptions

Number 1

BALANCED: *Pioneer, Original, Independent, Talented, Disciplined, Confident, Self-reliant, Courageous, Ambitious, Creative*

PASSIVE: *Lacks Drive, Stagnant, Opinionated, Obstinate, Weakness, Fearful*

NEGATIVE: *Self-centered, Egotistical, Controlling, Competitive, Rebel, Arrogant, Tyrant*

CAREERS: *CEO, Inventor, Entrepreneur, Leader, Visionary, Pioneer, Innovator, Politician, General*

LIFE PATH

You are a born leader and a trailblazer. You are here to master yourself and your abilities. You are an achiever of the highest order and your success is born through your keen intuition. Your integrity reins, as does your standard of quality. Your entrepreneurial skills come naturally and you are supported by your quick mental agility. Your magnetic personality enhances your leadership skills. People look to you for direction. One is a single number and therefore, you may feel lonely at times. One carries masculine qualities regardless of your gender. Gather your strength and courage because you will face challenges on your own and become a better human being through the experience. You have strong willpower and are determined to achieve all you set out to do. You may be alone much of the time due to your originality and fierce independence. You work well alone and are able to contemplate your next adventure. You adore a challenge and excel when beginning a new adventure. A life path number one teaches you to believe in yourself and to always stand up for yourself. Your competitive nature creates success, but needs to be held in check at times. Understanding we are all connected and serving humanity for the higher good is the greatest success of all. Embrace your individuality; become self-aware; believe in yourself; utilize your creative power; be a diplomatic leader; and master your aggression. Honor your strength, individuality and your independence.

DESTINY

Your destiny is to develop yourself and be a leader. Be courageous and embrace your independence; take the initiative to be original. Your ultimate goal is to develop a sense of self through your own will and determination. Have the courage to follow your original ideas and ambitions. Your success comes from self-reliance and your willingness to investigate new ideas and methods. You are destined to be a leader and manage others. Focus on your positive aspects and not what scares you. If you find yourself stuck, embarking on a self-improvement program is your best bet. Develop a connection to a higher source for inner direction. Achievement of your ambitions happens when you stay active and use your gifts wisely. There are no mistakes, only lessons on how to achieve success. You have a different way of viewing things. Honor your visions. Listen to your inner guidance and believe in yourself. Other's opinions are valuable, but the most reliable advice comes from within. Criticism is debilitating, in leadership of others and when directed at yourself. Life is an adventure to be experienced and explored. Lead by example, not by micromanaging, control or dominance. Be courageous and explore every avenue. Dullness is an enemy.

SOUL

Your independence is paramount. You are driven by your desire to be successful and lead others. You possess the courage to achieve whatever your heart desires. Your heart sings when you are discovering new avenues or exploring a new project. You adore blazing an undiscovered trail or begin a groundbreaking project. Live life with integrity and honesty and others will follow. Be a leader by example; temper your controlling nature. You are headstrong, willful, and ambitious, as well as independent. Your insightful wit and keen intelligence make you a good judge of character. Being a team player is not in your wheelhouse, but you do shine when you help others to succeed. Developing a relationship with a higher power enhances your adventures. Embrace your individuality and believe in yourself.

PERSONALITY

You are a dominant individual, who appears courageous and self-reliant. You have a dynamic personality and prefer standing out in a crowd. You see yourself as unique and despise being overlooked. You have a take charge personality and are always on the leading edge of any endeavor. You are seen as a pioneer who has original ideas. You may feel ahead of your time and spend much of your time alone. You can be intimidating, but others trust your leadership and guidance. "My way or the highway" is your mantra.

MATURITY

You learn leadership early in life and your strong ambitions lead you to positions of authority. Life experiences move you to greater inner strength and personal power. Your good memory and power of concentration teach you to stand in your convictions. You are independent to the core. Honoring your individuality creates a humanitarian leader. Your self-approval is more important than from a group. A connection to higher guidance will enhance your life experience. You have a broad vision, but can be single minded and set in your own ways. Lead by example, not by micromanaging, control or domination. Life experience gives you the courage to succeed.

CURRENT NAME

Having 1 energy in your current name enhances your independence, individuality, creativity and strength. Number one ignites your leadership skills and enables you to take control of your life. You have the ability to work autonomously or manage others in your own business.

BIRTHDAY 1, 10, 19, 28

You have strong leadership skills and enjoy taking control. Your determination and creativity fuel your achievements, but be sure to temper your arrogant and stubborn side. You will have to follow the rules sometimes. Be the "one of a kind" you are and express your individuality. Others will follow you.

MAJOR CYCLE

Formative

If your birth month is January or October, one is your first major cycle. As a one first cycle, you will learn independence and self-sufficiency. Leadership and decision-making skills are developed here and you will learn to build your self-confidence. You may find yourself alone often, or be lonely, because one is a solitary number. Find the courage to stand for what you believe in.

Progressive

If your birthday is on 1, 10, 19, or 28, you have one as a second cycle. During this 29-year progressive cycle, your self-confidence increases and you are able to master your leadership skills. This is the most productive cycle of your life, so look for entrepreneurial opportunities. Manage your loneliness and independence. This is a highly active time, so go with the flow as you stand on your own convictions. Believe in yourself.

Wisdom

If the year of your birth reduces to a number one, it will rule your third cycle. By now you've learned how to maintain your independence and learned many avenues to achieve success. This is also a time of self-discovery as you use the lessons from the previous cycles to master your leadership abilities. You are and will be seen as an authority. Others will follow you.

PINNACLE

This is a time to attain independence, self-sufficiency and originality. You will attract people who teach you to believe in yourself. "Do it myself" is your mantra. Summon the courage to take a leadership role and express your ideas. Allow your inner guidance to direct you; you have powerful "one" energy with you now. Temper your inner critic. Your perspective on life is formed in the first pinnacle during your formative years. In the later pinnacles, you learn leadership and all that entails; decision making, relationship building, problem solving, character development and mentoring.

CHALLENGE

You will have opportunities to stand up for yourself, believe in yourself and your ideals. You will find the courage to lead others as you stand on your own convictions. Self-discovery is paramount in the first challenge; you will know who you are as a person. The other challenge periods will build on your leadership skills and self-confidence. Seeking approval from others is tantamount to giving your power away. This is time to discover who you really are and not look outside to define yourself. Mistakes are nothing but lessons; learn from them. Now is the time to know your authentic self and discover your aspirations. Stay balanced, be true to yourself and honor your individuality.

ESSENCE

This is a time of new beginnings and forward focus. You may feel the desire to strike out on your own and test your independence. Many new ideas and opportunities enter every facet of your life. A high energy surge appears, so stay focused and true to yourself. New interests, new relationships, new career paths, and spiritual ideals are at the forefront. Release what's behind you and pay attention to your future. Let go of what isn't serving you and make room for new and better. You are required to be a leader. Take a stand, have the courage to challenge yourself. There are many demanding opportunities but with great effort, comes great rewards. Mistakes are nothing more than lessons to learn.

PERSONAL YEAR

New beginnings are in the forefront. The solitary number one means you are the primary focus here. You will feel the drive to create, build, and begin new projects. Use your visionary abilities to plant seeds for the next nine years. Everything you do this year affects the future. Ask yourself: "What is it I want to manifest in my life?" This is the time to concentrate on your future and actively participate in it. Have the courage and determination to create the person you want to become. Release everything not serving you and be open to a rebirth of new opportunities. Now is not the time to take a back seat or procrastinate. This is a time for independence and the courage to stand on your own two feet. Take care of yourself and be healthy. Improve yourself through personal growth classes. Expand your knowledge in every aspect of your life. The energy is with you and you'll find yourself in a leadership role. Your intuition is strong now, so step out and stretch yourself. This is an outer-focused number and time to put yourself in the public eye. A one year is highly active, busy, and full of opportunities. You can relax next year and watch the seeds you planted this year germinate. Concentrate on the positive aspects and you will see positive results. One carries a masculine quality, regardless of gender, so this is the year father issues may arise.

PERSONAL MONTH

New beginnings. Plant seeds, set your goals and intention for the next nine months. This is a busy month with many new projects. Have the courage to take the leadership role.

MISSING NUMBER

If an A, J or S does not appear in your name, you will have life lessons in leadership, independence, standing on your own and honoring your individuality. Without the one energy in your chart, you may be passive, have a lack of self-confidence and have an abundance of self-doubt. Your lesson is to know yourself and have the strength to honor your own convictions.

MULTIPLE NUMBER

With more than five ones in your name, you are determined and have a tendency to resist authority. You are a trailblazer and have interminable inner strength. You have great ambition and are highly competitive. You can be dominating, stubborn and impatient at times. You are a survivor, a warrior and avant-garde. It is okay to accept help once in a while.

PLANES OF EXPRESSION

Physical

You want to be in charge and have good leadership skills. You have little patience for the committee process. You are an achiever and thrive when challenged. You have strong opinions and rule your life according to them.

Mental

You are an innovator and not one to ask for advice. You learn quickly and can get bored easily. You are opinionated. You are honorable and have a solid moral compass. You can be impatient and prefer blazing a new trail instead of following traditional ones.

Emotional

You have strong feelings, but choose to either hide them or express them to make a point. Your self-control is exceptional and when anger does surface, it quickly dissipates. You can become attached to something or someone and may become possessive and domineering.

Intuitive

You are very intuitive and have sudden flares of insights. Any intuitive inspiration you receive is from a higher source and is a benefit if followed.

NUMBER 1 SUMMARY

Leader, entrepreneur, independent, individualistic. Wherever the one appears in your chart, it is all about you. You're the one with an abundance of ideas. You are not necessarily the one who completes the project, but you're the one with the innovative creations. You prefer the leadership role and hate to be ignored, overlooked, or missed. You want to be in the front of the crowd, facing them or leading them. There may be times when you feel like you're an outsider, but don't worry because you are dancing to your own drum and it is not necessary for you to fall into the crowd. Watch that your rebellious nature does not take hold or you become a control freak. Follow your heart and think outside the box.

One carries masculine qualities regardless of gender, and father issues may arise during a one year. This is the year to plant seeds for what you want to create in the next nine years. This is a time to think of everything you want to have, achieve, learn and be in the future. *You* are the focus this year and what you want is paramount. You have the one energy behind you energizing you to create what you want. Next year, you'll nurture these seeds and watch them grow, but this year is the time to get out there and take steps to create what it is you want.

Number 2

BALANCED: *Cooperation, Supportive, Sensitive, Mediation, Adaptable, Diplomatic, Considerate, Loving, Nurturing*

PASSIVE: *Indecisive, Meddling, Careless, Tactless, Over-sensitive, Apathetic, Shy*

NEGATIVE: *Deceptive, Critical, Moody, Jealous, Codependent, Cruel, Cowardly*

CAREERS: *Mediator, Counselor, Coach, Teacher, Intuitive, Negotiator, Diplomat*

LIFE PATH

Balance is the keyword here. Find harmony in all your endeavors. Cooperation, compromise, and patience reign. Your energy is calming, sensitive, and kind. Your abilities lie in helping others achieve their visions. Understanding your feelings and following your intuition will help you greatly in this harmonious life path. You are detail oriented and your deep insights are your strengths. You are the peacekeeper and born to relate to others. You avoid confrontation at all costs. You will find yourself in the role of mediator because you want everyone to cooperate. You have a strong intuition, and learning to trust it is most important. The more you tune into your intuition, the stronger it gets and the more it will guide you. You are best served when you surrender to your inner guidance. You are a strong support for those in your circle because of your innate counseling skills. Don't deny yourself and your needs while you make sure others' are met. Honor yourself. Set limits and boundaries. Two is the feminine number and therefore is receptive and has multiple supportive skills. You make an excellent partner because you are adaptable and cooperative. Stand up for yourself and learn to say no. Watch your over-sensitive and critical voice.

DESTINY

Your life's destiny is to create harmony, find balance, and seek cooperation. You have the ability to mediate, balance, harmonize, and negotiate any circumstances. You are a solid team player and your abilities make you an asset to any project. You are the supportive partner in all relationships. You are the quintessential diplomat. Collaboration and mediation are foremost in your life because you have the ability to see many different solutions to the same problem. Developing your intuition will pave the way to achieving your destiny. Surrender to your inner guidance and trust it to direct your life. Learning to be emotionally receptive will give you useful counseling skills. You are sensitive, gentle, compassionate and a consummate negotiator. Your sensitivity can become problematic; don't allow your inner critic to control you. Because you prefer the support position, you may not receive the accolades you deserve. Your destiny is to support others by finding peaceful resolutions. Develop your intuitive skills and follow your intuition to attain your life's mission to help others. You are better in a partnership than going solo.

SOUL

Your heart's desire is to have peace and harmony in all endeavors. You are kind, gentle, and generous. You are tactful about conveying truth and abhor criticism. You avoid confrontation at all costs and don't always stand up for yourself. Trusting your keen intuition and your own judgment is paramount for you. You can see both sides in any conflict and are a supportive companion. You are kind, gentle, patient, and bring calming energy to any situation. You prefer being in the background and unseen. You are not the star of the show, but your supportive contribution is invaluable. Be sure to stand up for your beliefs. Be decisive even when it is a challenge. Develop boundaries and stick to them.

Don't surrender your position just to avoid a confrontation. A relationship as a loving devoted partner is your heart's desire.

PERSONALITY

You are reserved, timid, and avoid the limelight. Cooperation is your mantra as you will always try to keep the peace. You are polite, diplomatic, and a good listener. Because of your diplomacy skills you can disarm a volatile situation. You are the quintessential peacekeeper. You are creative and pay attention to detail. You are an excellent companion who is supportive and has good listening skills. Others are attracted to you because of your grace and unthreatening nature. You are gentle, kind, and see harmony in all endeavors. You have a soothing personality and others look to you for compassion and understanding. You have a lovely sense of beauty and appreciate good taste. You may avoid confrontation at all costs and be seen as a weakling.

MATURITY

Your diplomacy skills are exemplary and you excel when cooperation is required. You are a humanitarian peacekeeper. Maintaining harmony is paramount. Your natural creativity shines in any endeavor, whether it is writing, art, music, or dance. Your intuition increases over the years and you may have psychic experiences. You are detail oriented and have a strong intuition. Following your inner guidance and strengthening your connection to the higher realms is the gift of the two maturity number. Harmonious relationships reign supreme as you honor inner peace. You always do well in a partnership or working in a group, rather than flying solo. Avoid other's critical judgments of you as you tend to take them too seriously.

CURRENT NAME

The energy of the two enhances your intuition. You are sensitive and aware of both sides of any conflict. Your supportive skills as a counselor and diplomat make you a valuable team member. Others look to you for guidance and understanding. You may not value yourself enough or the contribution you make.

BIRTHDAY 2, 11, 20, 29

The two birthday is the most harmonious birthday number of all. You are cooperative, intuitive and sensitive. You excel in relationships because you are the supportive partner. Two energy is the most supportive of all the numbers. Others look to you for guidance and understanding. Remember to meet your own needs and value your gifts. Temper your inner critic.

MAJOR CYCLE

Formative

If your birth month is February or November, your first cycle is number two. The energy of this cycle is slow and steady, so be patient with any developments. This is a time of learning cooperation and being a team player. Any relationships developed now are important. You may find yourself to be the peacekeeper in the family and among friends. Maintaining balance and equilibrium is paramount. A gentle vibration is in your life now and you have the opportunity to understand harmonious relationships and expand your creativity. This is the time to develop your intuition and trust it.

Progressive

If your birthday is 2, 11, 20, or 29, two energy rules your second major cycle. This is a time of harmony and equanimity. Maintain an equilibrium in your emotions. Find equanimity in your time between work and home. Balance your spiritual and intellectual pursuits. Balance others' needs with your own. Achievement is grounded in finding balance in every aspect of your life at this time. Relationships are paramount as you develop your supportive and counseling skills.

Wisdom

If the number two reigns your wisdom cycle, your harvest years will be full of love and companionship. You have become the pillar of the family and are now the peacekeeper in relationships. You are seen as the understanding one through your kindness and willingness to help. Your gentleness and supportive nature flow through you now. Your intuition is elevated and profound; surrender to it.

PINNACLE

Harmony, peace, and balance are at the forefront of this pinnacle. Your intuition is enhanced and you may be more sensitive to higher influences than in the past. Pay attention to detail and embrace your intuition. Relationships are important now as you learn cooperation, patience. You will take relating with others to another level. This is not a time for independence. Moderation, mediation and harmonizing with others is powerful energy for you now. Harmony is key now, especially between the inner and outer you. Balance your needs with others. Focus on your positive strengths and rewards will follow. Allow your intuition to guide you and surrender to a higher energy. Your energy is gentle and sensitive and important to a relationship. Your value and contributions may be overlooked; remember your self-worth comes from inside you. More than ever: silence your inner critic. You bring harmony and balance to the table. You flourish in beautiful and harmonious environments.

CHALLENGE

This is a sensitive period so be aware of feelings — yours and others. Be sensitive to your intuition and emotions, but not overly so. Watch your inner critic and don't take on other's criticism. You are the mediator and negotiator, not the instigator. Stay calm, create peace and harmony in your life. Humanity is best served when we all do this. Cooperation, not competition is the lesson, now more than ever. This challenge is an opportunity to learn to serve the highest good of all. This is not a time of selfish pursuits or achieving your own goals. Balance your feelings with others and do not surrender more of yourself to please others. Define your boundaries and stick to them. Don't shrink or hide yourself. Believe in yourself, trust your intuition and don't let your emotions run your life. You learn sensitivity, tact, diplomacy during this challenge.

ESSENCE

This is a slower development era when you are able to work on relationships. Cooperation, consideration, balance, and going with the flow are paramount. This is a time of new relationships and developing deeper connections which may lead to romance. You learn about being in partnership and working with others. You are the supportive member of the team, not the leader. You learn the value of working together and understand no one is an island. Your service is valued and you learn the importance of assisting in a goal that serves the greater good. Balance is paramount now, as it is a time of enhanced intuition and sense of awareness. Trust your higher guidance during this cycle more than ever. This is a time for decision making as life can change with new opportunities. Keep yourself grounded regularly and practice your patience during this slow and steady period. You appreciate beauty and find yourself in peaceful environments to keep you balanced. Don't let your emotions drag you down, keep your spirits high. You may need to support yourself, so find loyal friends who can help you through difficult times.

PERSONAL YEAR

Slow down, regroup, and listen to others. Reflect on the previous one year and take time to nurture the seeds you planted last year. This is not a year of outward achievements or attempting to row your boat upstream. Your personal power is subtle and indirect. Do not step out and create more goals on your own. Instead, this is a year of inner work and guidance. Focus on your personal growth. You need this introspection time and be grateful for the slower pace. Take this time to go inward and work on your own personal growth. Develop a relationship with your intuition. You will be more sensitive to others and may find you defer to them. You will need diplomacy and cooperation skills to negotiate with others. This is a time to relate to others and make compromises. Now is a time of slow growth and nurturing your aspirations of last year. Protect your ideas and attend to your creations; don't tell everyone about your plans. This is a favorable year for finding new love and or a new residence. Harmonize to a quiet tempo, relish the peace, and let the river guide your boat.

PERSONAL MONTH

Focus on details. Take care of the little things. Nurture the seeds planted last month. Cooperation in relationships is paramount after the previous one month of "It is all about me." This is an emotional month and may require your diplomacy skills.

MISSING NUMBER

Without the letters B, K, T in your name, you are required to learn the lessons of the two and adopt their characteristics. You may be impatient and tactless. Learn to filter your words and be more sensitive to feelings. Being oblivious to others' needs and being self-centered are attributes to overcome. You can be overly sensitive and take things personally. Learn cooperation, become a team player and have patience. Be mindful of good manners, strive for harmony and adapt diplomacy skills.

MULTIPLE NUMBER

If you have more than one number two in your name from the letters B, K, and T, you are a team player and work in harmony with others. You are patient, considerate and intuitive. You pay exceptional attention to detail and have a strong intuition. You are the quintessential peacemaker and prefer calm environments. Relationships are paramount to you. You may be shy, self-conscious, and too often, defer to others. You may be overly willing to please.

PLANES OF EXPRESSION

Physical

You are delicate and sensitive. You are the quintessential team player and are detail oriented. You prefer to be one of the crowd, rather than to stand on your own. Nature, especially water, is a calming influence. You are exceptionally adaptable and prefer doing things with a partner rather than alone. You may lack self-confidence and tend toward shyness.

Mental

You are the quintessential diplomat. You abhor confrontation and prefer everyone get along. You are deliberate in your thoughts but do not always express yourself. You are a good listener and work well in partnership. Decisions can be a challenge for you and you often vacillate.

Emotional

You can be overly sensitive and don't always hide your feelings. Emotional balance is essential to your well being and can be a challenge at times. You worry a lot and may become fearful and depressed. Understanding and communicating your emotions is a useful tool.

Intuitive

You are highly intuitive and more so than the average person. Learning to trust your insights is your best defense. Focus on spiritual and metaphysical pursuits to fully understand your intuitive abilities.

NUMBER 2 SUMMARY

You are gentle, receptive and you want everyone to get along. You are the mediator, the diplomat and the support. You don't want to be in front of the room as the number one; you are perfectly happy to sit in the back supporting them. Harmony and cooperation are your foundation and you make the best partner, but remember to stand up for yourself. You are highly intuitive and have insights far beyond other numbers, so be quiet and listen. You are a natural counselor, teacher, and have many creative abilities. You are empathic, kind, and your inner wisdom makes you the best friend.

Two carries feminine qualities regardless of gender, and in a two-year, mother issues may arise. This is a quiet year to relax and nurture the seeds you planted in the busy one year. This is a year of waiting and possible delays, so don't force your will. Get your relationships in order, use your many creative talents and your empathic gifts to be a support to your friends. Pay attention to detail and expand your meditation time, study a spiritual path and go inward. Rest, relax and listen to your inner guidance which is stronger during a two year.

Number 3

> **BALANCED:** *Creative, Enthusiastic, Optimistic, Artistic, Spiritual, Communicative, Intuitive*
>
> **PASSIVE:** *Self Centered, Idle, Scattered, Unforgiving, Lacks Focus*
>
> **NEGATIVE:** *Jealous, Intolerant, Superficial, Extravagant, Vain, Trivial, Complaining*
>
> **CAREERS:** *Artist in any medium, Writer, Painter, Motivational Speaker, Sales, Actor*

As a number three, you are creative, fun loving, social, spontaneous, optimistic, enthusiastic, artistic, and the quintessential communicator. You are attracted to luxury and all things beautiful. Abundance and opportunities naturally flow to you. Freedom is paramount. You are capable of deep love. You can be self-centered and lazy at times and lean toward the extravagant. Gossip is your thing and you can superficially link your ego to your artistic prowess. Three is the marriage of the masculine and feminine. Three combines the initiating force of the one with the nurturing two energy for manifestation.

LIFE PATH

Your purpose is to live joyfully and uplift humanity. You are creative, spontaneous, and enjoy life to the fullest. Your abundant imagination and enthusiasm are inspirational to everyone you meet. Use your magnetic personality and optimistic outlook to inspire others. Share your endless creativity with the world as another form of expressing your joy. You are the quintessential communicator and destined for expressing yourself. Learn to use your words and speak your truth. You are a visual and use this talent to express yourself through any art medium. You know laughter is healing and through your boundless happiness, you bring joy to others. Always optimistic and resilient, you overcome many obstacles. When you express your creative ideas and speak from your heart you are fulfilling your life purpose. Make everything you do an expression of your joy and demonstrate it in everything you do. Success will follow you through self discipline and commitment. Money comes easy to the lucky number three, but you are prone to let it slip through your fingers easily. Lighten up, be happy. Don't let your sensitivity to criticism or sarcasm get the best of you. You can fall prey to negativity and laziness. Remember there is power in your words, so gossip, exaggeration, and complaints can derail you. You have a powerful resilience to recover from any setbacks. When you use your endless talents to uplift humanity, success, and a joyful life are your rewards.

DESTINY

Your destiny is fulfilled when you encourage and inspire others. Use your optimism and enthusiasm to energize and uplift all you meet. You are here to demonstrate how to live joyfully so others can learn from you. A world of endless joy and creativity is waiting for you to manifest it in the present. Communicate with your inner child and create a life of childlike wonderment. Know your emotions and learn to express them through your powerful gift of communication. Your creative imagination is at the heart of the number three, however, lack of self-discipline may inhibit your success. Focus, commitment, and diligence are a solid foundation on which to build your creative talents. Ideas flow to you like the air you breathe and it is imperative you don't get lost in the creation of them. Choose and move — select one idea and see it through to fruition. Boundaries are a good structure for you and limiting your focus to finish a project will ensure success. You are destined to express yourself through speaking and writing. You are a catalyst for change, so integrate all your talents to help humanity. You are multi-talented and have unlimited ideas so stay focused and do not scatter or waste them. Money comes to you easily as does love and romance. Watch your finances, though, as you may squander your resources. You enjoy the good life and are not made for heavy work. You are impulsive and search for momentary gratification. Use your determination for success to focus and organize, then you'll achieve your destiny.

SOUL

Your heart's desire is to create joy in your life and for those around you. Your enthusiasm reigns supreme when you are happy and outgoing. You love life and are instantly romantic; very little can bring you down. Playfulness and enjoyable experiences make your heart sing. Lighten up and laugh whenever the opportunity arises. Be creative and inspirational to encourage those near you. You know your emotions and are able to articulate them although you prefer to stay on the surface rather than dig too deep. Your verbal skills are superior and you'll enjoy any career which allows for full self-expression. Discipline and commitment are necessary to successfully express your limitless imagination. Being grounded will allow you to soar to greater heights. Your abundant joyful demeanor is infectious. Allow your creative imagination to soar, but develop self-discipline to succeed. You tend toward happiness rather than pragmatism. Your mind fluctuates and you can be too accommodating at times. Use your words to inspire joy in others and your heart is fulfilled.

PERSONALITY

The three personalities are magnetic, fun-loving, and excellent communicators. You are charming, entertaining, often attractive, and use your gifts to be the center of attention. Your contagious joyful outlook is an inspiration to others. People love being in your energy and you are at home as the center of attention. Keep it up and expand your vision of a happy life. Beauty and luxury appeal to you and you enjoy the finer qualities in life. As an extroverted socialite you are optimistic, witty, and have a great sense of humor. You tend to fall in love quickly, loving the romance, but when that fades, may move on just as quickly. Work on building lifelong relationships so you can delve deep rather than have only surface conversations all the time. Remember diligence

41

and focus will create success. You may tend toward exaggeration and fall prey to jealousy and gossip.

MATURITY

You have an elevated imagination and exquisite artistic talent. You are most joyful when you are using all your gifts to bring joy and happiness to the world. It can be an easy life if you focus on the positive and allow abundance. A magical zest for life allows you to create to your heart's desire. Be spontaneous and do not repress your talents as you can become cranky and depressed. You are sensitive and expressive and have a true gift of communication. Watch you don't waste your energy on idle talk, but rather use your excellent communication skills to create something of lasting value. You cherish your friendships and are successful with money when you balance your energies. You may have had a challenging childhood, but the second half of your life is easier and filled with joy.

CURRENT NAME

You have numerous creative talents and the dynamic ability to express yourself through speaking or the written word. You are able to enjoy life and have many friends. Your words carry weight, so watch them wisely. Gossip, criticism, and exaggeration are not good for you or anyone else.

BIRTHDAY 3, 12, 21, 30

You are a born communicator and can express yourself through the spoken or written word. Three is truly a lucky number. Your creative gifts abound as you are joyful inspiration to others. You are optimistic and friendly and usually see the glass half full. A foundation of discipline will aid your success. Keep your focus and finish your projects; you will never get very far stopping midway.

MAJOR CYCLE

Formative

If your birthday falls in March or December, 3 rules your first major cycle. This is a time of self-expression and exploring your talents as a communicator. Discover your creative abilities in this cycle and rewards abound. This is a time to focus on your creative expression, whether it is writing, art, music or dance. You enjoy the limelight and are entertaining to your many friends. Enjoy having fun, but be sure partying doesn't take all your attention. Stay focused and finish your commitments.

Progressive

If your birthday is 3, 12, 21, or 30, your second cycle is ruled by three. Explore, develop, and express your many talents. You are required to increase your focus and commitment. This is when you can hone your artistic skills. Honor your emotions and express your truth. This is a time of many friends who adore your charming personality. Balance your creative side with structure and commitment for a rewarding cycle.

Wisdom

The vibration of number three in your harvest cycle brings joy in all you do. Self-expression in all forms: writing, dance, art, and music. Your aging years are full of friends and social engagements. Money flows naturally to you so enjoy this freedom and use your creative talents. A positive attitude will ensure success in your older years, so keep a higher vibration and be a magnet for all you desire. This is the most delightful of all wisdom cycles.

PINNACLE

This is a time for fun and creative pursuits. If you didn't know you were creative before, now is the time to explore it. Do not judge your projects: creativity is about the creating and not being overly critical. Discover fun adventures; maybe look at joyful experiences you had as a child. Lighten up and giggle. Discipline takes a backseat and enjoying life's pleasures is the driving force. If a three pinnacle is early in life, you are to embrace your emotions and learn to express yourself. This is a time to nurture your imagination and creative side. During the progressive and harvest years, you'll learn balance is paramount. Learning to speak from the heart and express your emotions will see you through this joyful pinnacle. This is a highly imaginative time when you are called to encourage and inspire others. Have a positive outlook and let your optimism be your driving force. Stay focused and committed lest you scatter all your energies. Refine your many artistic abilities and express yourself. Diligence and structure are required with three energy to achieve success. The challenge is to find something which brings you joy and the work becomes play. Life may be easier during this pinnacle so take care not to wallow in self-indulgence and become lazy. Temper your impulses. Create, play, imagine.

CHALLENGE

This is a time for knowing your emotions and expressing them. Uncover your inner joy. Lighten up. Smile. Allow yourself to laugh. Allow joy into your life. Don't take things so seriously. Silence your inner critic: it is debilitating and damaging. Your words are powerful and affect all aspects of your life. Be aware of your speech. Be positive. This is an expansive era and a time to learn to live a happy life. Open your imagination channel, and express your creativity through any form of art, regardless of size or media. Paint a mural or plant flowers. Sing or dance or do both. Honor your feelings and don't deflect. But don't get lost in your feelings either. Overcome your self-doubt and build up your self-confidence. You face the negative aspects of the three vibration and all that entails. Exaggeration, gossip, scattered focus are in your energy field now and you may create superficial relationships. Delve deep into your emotions even though this is especially a challenge now. Write down your emotions in a journal. Express yourself even if it is only to you. Value your own creativity. You may find yourself alone much of this challenge period. Put yourself out there and trust you will find your tribe. Use your creative energy to inspire a loving, positive atmosphere full of joy.

ESSENCE

This is a sweet era of creative expression in all forms. Your words pour out of you as creativity abounds in writing, art, dance, and design. Love comes to you in this highly emotional and social era, so enjoy life. A time of manifestation and opportunities abound for advancement both personally and in your career. You can accomplish a lot during this highly creative time. You will have occasions to witness your own individuality and uniqueness. Don't scatter your energy, stay focused and explore one creative idea at a time. Your ideas have merit and success comes when you focus your energy to create something of lasting value. Keep your positive outlook to attract abundance and more joy. Keep your negativity in check and watch your finances. Money flows to you, but it can flow away just as easily. Be aware of emotions not resolved as they may appear now. Commitment and discipline will always balance any three energy, regardless of where it appears on your chart.

PERSONAL YEAR

Creativity reigns supreme in a three year. Writing, speaking, drama and any artistic endeavor are excellent pursuits now. Expand your imagination, manifest your dreams, explore the unexplored to reach new heights. This is the time of expanding your horizons and personal growth. More social engagements are likely this year and more relationships. Delve deeper into your emotions. Knowing your emotions and learning to express them is important now. Learn to express yourself first and then frolic in your imagination. Use your creative power to have fun this year. Watch your tendency for extravagance, but there is no harm in imagining having beautiful possessions. Negativity breeds drama and chaos, so keep to the positive side. Discipline and commitment always balance the creative three energy and engaging them will return great rewards. Enjoy your creative imagination and you will have a joyful year before the four-year energy shifts into hard work.

PERSONAL MONTH

Creative juices pour out of you now, and you'll find new ideas to create abundance. This is a playful time, but keep it simple and stay focused. Redecorate, redesign a project, write a story and dance.

MISSING NUMBER

If C, L or U does not appear in your name, you may have difficulty communicating or expressing your feelings. Your life lesson is to freely expound on the joy of living; lighten up and be happy. You may have antisocial tendencies and work too much. Lighten up and look at the positive side of life. Control your moodiness and temper your complaints and negativity. Go out and do something fun. Silence your inner critic.

MULTIPLE NUMBER

If you have a number 3 three or more times in your name from the letters C, L and U, you are highly artistic and imaginative. You are a creative thinker, good speaker and love music. You have supreme writing and speaking skills and are inspiring to others. You value luxury and manual work is not in your wheelhouse. You tend toward boredom easily. Procrastination works against you as does leaning to the extreme in any area. The need for talking to hear yourself speak, extravagant spending, or demanding the spotlight should all be held in check.

PLANES OF EXPRESSION

Physical

You are happy, charismatic, creative, and have a good sense of humor. Your childlike approach may leave you scattered and with a lack of discipline. You may quit too early and leave many unfinished projects. You are sociable and playful, but can have temperamental outbursts. A strong sense of structure and discipline will help you greatly in your life.

Mental

You are open and friendly and have a vivid imagination. You see humor in just about everything. You tend to scatter your thoughts, projects, and your own energy. You are a true communicator able to articulate your thoughts and feelings. You are a gifted artist especially in any form based on words. Discipline and focus are necessary to balance your life.

Emotional

You are a joyful human being with a warm heart. You tend toward the romantic and likely found refuge in your own fantasies as a child. You can be jealous and demanding.

Intuitive

You are highly intuitive and connect to the higher realms easily. An inspiration to all you meet, your gift of communication is a benefit to all. Your seemingly endless creativity is a joy for all to witness.

NUMBER 3 SUMMARY

Creator, Communicator, Talented Artist. Joyful, Lucky. You are the happy one who enjoys life and loves to have fun. Finding your perfect avenue for self-expression is paramount. Whether an artist or musician, you have varied talents. Understanding your emotions and learning how to express them is your life lesson. Lucky number three is true for you. One is the masculine, two is the feminine, and three is the marriage of both: the holy trinity. Creation is your fuel and you are gifted with many opportunities to express yourself. You'll give birth to many ideas, so watch you don't get scattered. You love to talk and your words have power, so don't waste them on idle gossip.

A three year brings creative energy to you, so express yourself. You'll want to converse more, enjoy life more, and express your emotions. Get in touch with how you're feeling and then articulate them. Ideas flow freely, but don't get lost in the creation, lest you become scattered. Persevere and see your creations through to fruition. Don't procrastinate or get lazy; you won't always have the creative energy flowing through you. This should be a great year for you, money and ideas flow freely. Prioritize your goals and follow through. You'll have a lot to show at the end of the three year.

Number 4

BALANCED: *Loyal, Diligent, Organized, Honors Integrity, Dedicated, Dependable, Service, Traditional, Methodical, Stable. Practical. Efficient*

PASSIVE: *Lazy, Argumentative, Stubborn, Passive-Aggressive, Dull, Repressed*

NEGATIVE: *Intolerant, Vulgar, Combative, Aggressive, Rigid, Insensitive, Workaholic*

CAREERS: *Dedicated employee, Teacher, Builder, Accountant, Scientist*

LIFE PATH

You will follow the workers path. Solid and stable, you understand what it means to follow rules and be loyal. When you fully understand the definitions of reliable and responsible, you can begin to build your career. You are organized, efficient, and being on time is important to you. Everything you accomplish in life is built on the foundations you create, so have a clear intention. You are the most dependable and steady of all the numbers. You are the tortoise, slow and steady, not one to race ahead or cut corners. Dedication is key and you thrive on bringing order to chaos which makes you an outstanding manager. A four life path teaches you the importance of creating a secure foundation on which to build. When you are following your life path, you are creating your dreams on earth. You understand the value of perseverance, organization, and commitment and know the value of those characteristics. The number fours are the worker bees. You can take an idea and bring it into fruition. Take time to honor your success. You are the "nose to the grindstone" character who, in a harmonious life, is patient and loyal. You are organized, dedicated, and have a good amount of integrity. Looking outside the box can be a challenge at times and you sometimes see the glass half full. Staying positive and flexible will give you more opportunities to achieve your dreams. You can be narrow minded, stubborn, and prefer your own methods. At the far end of the scale, you are too serious, lack sensitivity, and can be a workaholic. Take time to celebrate your accomplishments. The number four vibration can signify health issues, so take special care of your body.

DESTINY

Your destiny is to bring stability and order to the world. Your diligence creates strong foundations on which to build a solid life. With stellar organizational skills, you are the consummate manager in all aspects of your life. You bring substance and meaning to your projects. You are practical, steady, and have the stamina to achieve any goal. You know which obstacles to overcome to achieve success. You are the quintessential manager and know how to delegate responsibilities to ensure the job gets done. You have excellent managerial skills, but micromanaging will pollute your reputation.

Security is paramount in your existence and with a strong foundation under you, success is your destiny. Always the threat of being a workaholic, be sure to schedule rest, relaxation and rejuvenation. You are resilient and can endure the most stressful project, but you are not a machine. Take time to enjoy life. Watch your health and take care of your body. Remember to see the glass half full some of the time. Celebrate your accomplishments.

SOUL

Your heart's desire is to always be organized and have order in your life. You have a practical plan to ensure everything runs efficiently. You require schedules in your world and always having a list makes you happier. Having clear boundaries and understanding what's expected eases your heart. You like having control and being the supervisor to accomplish every goal on which you set your heart. Spontaneous surprises aren't your thing, you prefer a predictable steady pace. Your seriously practical side prevents you from buying frivolous gifts or tending toward the romantic. You thrive when your foundation is secure and are a most dependable and loyal friend. Remember there is joy in life too and don't take everything seriously. Being adaptable and able to accept the unexpected will benefit you in the long run.

PERSONALITY

You appear to the world as a solid, honest member of humanity who follows the rules. A practical and sensible citizen who leans toward the conservative side of most affairs. Diligent and prudent, you are a most sought-after worker. Reliability and responsibility are the characteristics of a stellar employee. Being frivolous and extravagant are not in your wheelhouse as your focus is down to earth. You can appear aloof to some and prefer your own judgment.

MATURITY

If your youth taught you the value of diligence and discipline, this four maturity will bring expansion and refinements. Having a foundation of self-discipline and practical application, you know how to achieve your dreams. You desire to contribute; to be a part of something substantial. Your organizing skills and your necessary back up plan are sure elements of a successful organization. Characteristics such as reliability, responsibility, and dedication make you a stellar employee. Appreciate your skills and the exceptional employee you are. The most hardworking and frugal of all the numbers, you have the skills to facilitate any given task. Having a four maturity number ensures you never retire, instead preferring to use your talents to make a contribution. Your way is always the best, according to you and you can be seen as domineering and self-righteous. Take care of any health issues and spend time working at something which brings you joy.

CURRENT NAME

The number four vibration adds dedication and perseverance to your chart. Your organizational skills and determination to achieve success increase when you have the four energy. You'll feel the need to have a strong foundation under you to achieve your dreams.

BIRTHDAY 4, 13, 22, 31

Perseverance, discipline, and commitment to achieve success are your gifts if born on a four day. You see the necessary steps to face obstacles, and are trusted to do the honest thing. You are a loyal and committed partner, but being romantic isn't your strong suit.

MAJOR CYCLE

This is a working cycle. Create order and build foundations for your future. Pragmatism reigns in every aspect of your life now. Diligence is required for a successful career and equal attention directed at home and community. Prudence and frugality are good stones for a solid foundation.

Formative

If you are born in April, your early years prepare you for hard work and learning the value of security. Stability, responsibility, integrity, and the value of a strong foundation are taught in this cycle. Understanding slow and steady is the best plan, patience and perseverance will be rewarded. Not much attention is paid to process emotions during this early period of life. It is a solid cycle to learn positive ethics and values on which to build a strong foundation for a successful life.

Progressive

If your birthday is 4, 13, 22, or 31, your progressive years will be full of hard work to build a solid foundation for success. Commitment and determination to succeed will ensure you achieve your goals. You have the opportunity to become a pillar of the community and the center of your family if you keep your nose to the grindstone and be responsible. This can be a demanding cycle, but also a rewarding one. Be sure to balance your diligence with relaxation and rejuvenation.

Wisdom

The number four vibration in your wisdom cycle produces years of security and stability. Keep your finances safe, maintain your organizational skills, and you will continue to provide for your family. You will likely not retire because you prefer to remain active. Your health would be the only obstacle preventing you from keeping a work schedule.

PINNACLE

A four pinnacle during any stage in life means you learn structure, discipline and hard work. This is the time to build solid foundations to last you a lifetime. Endurance, stamina and patience are needed to learn the lessons of a four pinnacle. Plan, organize and set up systems to create future success. Methodical in your movements, use your practical side to put your ideas and dreams into reality. You are creating your space in the world. This is a demanding pinnacle which requires discipline, diligence, and commitment to see your objectives through to fruition. You build your inner strength and see the value in it. This is not a leisure time. You work hard now, but you see the rewards of your diligence continually through your lifetime. Money, schedules, and efficiency teach you now. Limitations and regulations may leave you frustrated, but the qualities you create now are worth the struggle. Perseverance and diligence payoff. A four pinnacle early in life means you may be influenced through financial limitations of your parents.

CHALLENGE

You are to learn about rules, structure and the benefits of building a solid foundation. Diligence, organization, frugality and practicality are the boundaries. You learn how to contend with restrictions and limitations. A methodical and organized approach to your projects is needed now. Dedicated and committed to completion are in the foundation to master

53

a four challenge. This is a time for patience, working with the natural flow, and being practical. There are limitations in this period and it is prudent to keep your self-righteousness in check. You learn valuable lifetime lessons under this challenge and best to honor what you know. Despite the obstacles, staying positive will ease the challenge. Being flexible and adaptable will ease your struggle. Take care of your body and deal with any health issues as they arise.

ESSENCE

Structure and organization rule this essence to create a solid foundation for your life. Be responsible with money, health, career, and family. Be disciplined in all you endeavor. Pay attention to the details and do a reality check. Face unresolved issues and settle them. This includes family, career, personal relationships and your health. Do not procrastinate. This is a slower period with limitations and requires commitment and diligence to live within them. Moments routinely spent in quiet contemplation will give you perspective. This is a time to create boundaries and live with limitations. Remain positive and be appreciative for everything in your life.

PERSONAL YEAR

This is your year to build a solid foundation for the next nine years. Structure and discipline are required this year to reset your life and prepare for the time ahead. Build a foundation solidly enough for you to plan your future. Clear out, repurpose, and throw away any excess clutter. Last year was one to create ideas and brainstorm. You are more focused this year. Use it to put those creative ideas into form. Next year is one of great freedom and expansion and requires a solid foundation. This is your year for discipline. Learning discipline now will benefit you the rest of your life. Pay attention to details; take care of issues as they arise. Organization at home and work is required to secure a stable future. Remodel your home, finish incomplete projects as you have the four energy supporting your focus. Unresolved family issues may arise and now is the time to process them. Legal issues may appear so be patient, but do not procrastinate. This is not the year to take great risks; wait until next year. Take care of your health during this four year as health issues may occur. Determination and commitment will see you through this hard-working year. Remain positive and follow the rules for a rewarding year. A four year is challenging at the time but if you focus, do your work, you will reflect back on it with satisfaction and gratitude.

PERSONAL MONTH

Organization, discipline and diligence this month. Take care of your health through diet and exercise. Bring your creations from last month into material form. Finish a project. Reset your foundation for the expansive five month ahead.

MISSING NUMBER

If D, M, or V does not appear in your name, life will give you lessons in discipline and organization. You may be impractical, unmotivated, and tend to procrastinate. Commitment and discipline may not be in your wheelhouse. You may feel lost at times and it is important for you to understand diligence and structure are necessities for a successful future. It's imperative you build a secure foundation on which to create your life. Take care of your body and be responsible, structured, and focused. Rewards appear and dreams are realized when you utilize these skills.

MULTIPLE NUMBER

If you have one or two fours in your name from D, M or V, you are diligent, responsible, and committed to your goals. You are determined to overcome all obstacles to achieve them. Organization is your foundation. You relish in hard work and are detail oriented. You are the quintessential loyal employee. You are solid and loyal; your family leans on your stability and sound judgment. Three or more fours in your name can bring too much structure and routine to your life. You can be rigid, not open to new ideas and tedious. Learn to be patient, flexible, and adaptable. Be social, join a club, and learn to relax.

PLANES OF EXPRESSION

Physical

You are meticulous about your appearance as you are most things. You are a skillful builder and commit to seeing a project to fruition. You are determined, pragmatic and organized. You are a diligent worker who is loyal and honest. You can be solemn and silent and at times, rigid and stubborn.

Mental

You like an established order to life, preferring routines and regimes. You adapt a practical approach to life and are naturally organized. You are loyal and obedient, willing to follow orders to the letter. Watch you don't lose yourself in the details. You can be domineering and demanding.

Emotional

You adapt a calm demeanor and prefer to appear in control of your emotions at all times. You may not be in touch with your own emotions and are uncomfortable when others express theirs.

Intuitive

You may not be in touch with your intuition but you have one. If you connect to it, you'll realize it is a practical tool in your wheelhouse.

NUMBER 4 SUMMARY

Four is the worker-bee number. You prefer things to be a certain way — your way — and depend on them staying the same way. You love rules and boundaries and adhere to them. Routine, structure, and discipline are in your wheelhouse. You are practical, dependable, and dedicated to getting the job done. When you want something completed, call a four. You work better with an organized plan and are a gifted delegator. Your rigidity might impede your ability to adapt to change and learning to go with the flow will make you easier to get along with.

A four year is a time to settle down and build a solid foundation. Life will bring lessons this year to encourage you to set boundaries and create structure.

You'll work extra hard to lay the groundwork, bottom line. Persevere and focus to get the job done. Take care of your health and stabilize your life. Make your home repairs, organize the office and take the year seriously. The next year as a five year requires a solid foundation and can be chaotic if you haven't worked hard in your four year.

Number 5

> **BALANCED:** *Freedom Seeker, Curious, Progressive, Flexible, Adventurous, Fun, Witty, Diverse, Energetic*
>
> **PASSIVE:** *Fears Change, Irresponsible, Hypocritical, Restless, Demands Rules, Ignores Life Lessons*
>
> **NEGATIVE:** *Overindulgent, Addictions, Abuse of Freedom, Ignores Rules, Disregards Values*
>
> **CAREERS:** *Motivational Speaker, Sales, Public Relations, Teacher, Coach, Inventor*

LIFE PATH

You are a true freedom-seeker and quintessential adventurer. Expansion is the foundation for your life. You are a lover of life and want to experience every aspect of it. Born an explorer in every realm, you want to try everything once. Yours is a life learned through experience and you're not one to follow the advice of others. Travel and promotion are excellent uses for your skillset, or any career within the public eye. You are a quick learner and acquire a variety of skills through your many experiences. Sudden change rules your life and gives you surprising opportunities. Flexibility and adaptability are your best tools to navigate the variety of experiences you'll have. You are a sensual being and desire to explore through all your senses: smelling, touching, hearing, seeing, and tasting everything life has to offer. Inconsistency and change are the only constants. See life as a series of adventures without judgment and fully learn from them. You are the trailblazer, the one who breaks old conventions and creates a new path. You are the searcher bee, the one to discover new flowers to pollinate. A talented communicator and gifted motivator. makes you an excellent teacher or speaker. To achieve mastery however, you need focus and commitment. Moderation and discipline guarantee stability and success. Live in the moment, do not focus your attention on the past or your future. Watch your impulses. Be careful not to scatter your many energies or get lost in your addictions. Stick with something; cultivate an idea to fruition to realize what you can achieve. You don't need another unfinished project. The possibilities are infinite. Sharing with others the lessons from your life experience is your true reward. The number five is all about expansion, change, and freedom. Live in the moment. You are multi-talented, energetic and have adventures. You are a curious freedom seeker who has a rebellious nature and prefers the unconventional. You avoid routine and abhor the mundane. Your quick wit and charming nature enhance your magnetic personality. To the extreme, you can be fearful, moody, restless, overindulgent, scattered, overextended, and caught up in addiction. Variety spices your life. Moderation is the key to balancing five energy. It is wise for you to learn from others and not have to experience everything personally.

DESTINY

Freedom is at the core of your existence. Your life's mission is to experience freedom and adapt to change. Life is a learning process and your destiny is to embrace freedom to explore it. Live life to the fullest is your mantra, so be the explorer and learn all you can. You will meet many people in your global travel adventures. Your youthful enthusiasm is attractive to others and you'll have many friendships. Your innate sensuality ensures many love relationships. You are multitalented and do well at anything you attempt. You have the ability to succeed at anything you choose, but need diligence and discipline to achieve mastery. The more grounded you are, the higher you can soar. You will learn from your choices and mistakes, so value each experience. Liberation and adventure are at the nucleus of your being. Do not waste your acquired talent or ignore your passions. Take risks, follow your heart, push the limits of foundation, and think outside the box. Your perspective on life does not include boundaries, the status quo, or the way things have always been done. Your vision blazes a new trail and lets go of outdated thought and judgmental views. Remain positive and trust in the Universe. Everything works out for a reason. Your true destiny is served when you share with others all you have learned.

SOUL

Your heart's desire is to be free of any restriction or outdated mindset. Freedom at all costs. Your passion is adventure in every aspect of your life. You enjoy unpredictability and thrive when you are free of limitations. You relish being different from others and prefer foraging a new path over a well worn road. Your passion for variety is predominant and you may have difficulty committing to anything. Change, adventure, and sensual romance are deep in your heart. You adore variety and abhor the mundane. Stimulation is your fuel; routine stalls your engine. Your enthusiasm is contagious as you encourage others to be more adventurous and willing to grow. Having choices is paramount, allowing the future to unfold and learning from your mistakes. Use your five senses to experience all of life's offerings and you'll know your true heart's desire. Be careful not to lose yourself in sensory gratification so much so you ignore your ambitions.

PERSONALITY

You are charming, sexually attractive, and have a witty personality. Others see your adventuresome spirit and admire you for it. Variety is the spice of life and you seek experiences to prove it. Freedom is paramount with your adventurous spirit. You are naturally outgoing and adaptable. Changing careers, partners, homes, or hobbies is easy for you. You are a forward thinker and spirited communicator: a true inspiration to all you meet. You have the ability to learn easily and therefore have knowledge of a wide range of subjects. Skimming the surface and having superficial knowledge can only get you so far. Your adaptability and chameleon-like character give you the skill to make the most of every opportunity. You don't like accumulating possessions as they can tie you down. Your desire for travel and adventure may pull you away from your obligations, so remember that being grounded and centered will allow you to adventure farther. You can be seen at times as anxious and impatient.

MATURITY

Life is thrilling and full of variety. Your curiosity rewards you with diversity and many options. You are a resourceful freedom-seeker and natural risk taker. Anything new fuels your independent spirit and you see life as one great adventure. There are always other places to go, things to do, people to meet. You learn to let go enough that you can expand your freedom to be different. You have a quick wit and are attractive to others. Your wisdom and knowledge expand; your creativity and individuality grow stronger. Your natural gift for communication directs you to share all your life lessons. Release your attachment to the past to live in the moment. Harness your restless nature and your innate escape reflex. Your life experiences teach you to be more open and flexible in your later years. Do not believe you are too old for new experiences, ever. More freedom comes to you in your later years, but don't scatter your energies. Hold back your fears and encourage yourself to take the risk. Be outrageous, persevere and expand your self-image. Be patient.

CURRENT NAME

The five energy brings communication and promotion skills. Sales and being in the public eye serve you. Adaptability and flexibility carry the five vibration as well as risk taking and adventurous spirit. Expand your thinking and be confident in your choices.

BIRTHDAY 5, 14, 23

You adore travel and adventure. Your innate curiosity for life makes you a global traveler. You are multi-talented; a gifted communicator, salesperson, educator, or advisor. You work well with others provided there are few restrictions and you are free to do as you please. A natural promoter, you are witty and adaptable. Learning something new comes easily and rewards you with a varied skill set and numerous talents. It is wise for you to learn discipline and structure at a young age or you may be subject to a superficial life. Watch your addictions and be careful not to overindulge in food, drugs, sex, or alcohol. Your health is more important than instant gratification. Learn to temper your impulses and try to be more patient. Live in the moment and keep your focus on the here and now.

MAJOR CYCLE

Formative

If you are born in May, your first life cycle is five. The five energy brings a freedom loving cycle. Change, change, and more change in every aspect of life. Time to find adventure and seek new opportunities. Take risks, expand your experiences, but don't get scattered. In this first cycle of life, you learn all about freedom. Learn life is exciting if you desire adventure and change or learn life is a challenge if structure and stability rule you. This is an era of freedom and too much at a young age may create precarious situations. Structure tempers this expansive cycle and adaptability is the bottom line.

Progressive

If your birthday is 5, 14, or 23, you are in a rapidly progressive cycle. Change permeates all avenues of your life: home, career, leisure activities. The number five is freedom energy and releases you from life's burdens. Adventure awaits, so seek new experiences and don't be afraid to take risks. You are learning life's lessons about managing freedom. Too much freedom and irresponsibility may develop. Not enough freedom and oppression squeezes out your life force. Learn all you can in this expansive cycle and remember to share your wisdom with others.

Wisdom

Your harvest years are expansive and adventurous. Your freedom loving spirit is in charge and if you're financially prepared, it is time to travel the world. Forever youthful and energetic, now is the time to realize your dreams. Try something new or do something you said you never would. Break an old habit.

PINNACLE

Change is the essence of the five pinnacle. Be flexible, adaptable, and release all restrictions. This is a time of exploration and adjusting to unpredictable experiences which can come at a rapid pace. This expansive period is about experimentation and learning. Be open to anything coming your way; read a new book, take a masterclass, discover a new art medium. Seemingly insignificant events can take root and blossom during this period. Seize an opportunity for the experience and do not doubt it or question why. Change is constant and usually unexpected, so this may be an uncomfortable era at times. Do not waste this opportunistic energy flow hiding at home, but rather step out in the world and promote yourself. Stay positive, release self-doubt, and propel yourself outward. Try something new everyday. Remain grounded, however, and resist the impulse to escape responsibility. Be aware you do not become a permanent nomad. A superficial life is not a rewarding one, so cultivating your talents and accepting some limitations are necessary. Balance and moderation will ensure a successful era. Adapt and go with the flow.

CHALLENGE

Mastering the five energy is at the heart of this challenge. Your desire for freedom and expansion may outweigh other ambitions. You may be close to becoming a nomadic vagabond. Senses are enhanced, be aware of overindulgence in your addictions with food, sex, drugs, alcohol, work, or gambling. Change reigns supreme, but don't change for the sake of change. See projects through to completion. You have a a tendency to scatter your abilities and get caught up in the whirlwind of change and superficial pursuits. Balance and moderation are key. Fulfilling obligations while embracing freedom is the lesson. Free yourself from limiting behaviors but don't ignore responsibilities. Focus your energy and attention for success. Develop and maintain long lasting relationships, don't discard them just because you may be going through a rough patch. Stability, discipline, and consistency manage this free-wheeling time. A balanced sense of freedom and responsibility bring harmony to this challenge.

ESSENCE

This is a progressive period with limited restrictions. A time to release your past, focus forward and explore new opportunities and adventures. Eliminate anything old or whatever holds you back; your future holds the key. This is an intensely powerful time; your abilities are heightened, especially your communication skills. Opportunities appear as if from nowhere, so be ready for sudden surprises. Expansive personal growth is possible through meeting new people, career opportunities or traveling the world. Use this new found freedom responsibly and maintain your center. Do not scatter your talents or lose sight of your life goals. Moderation of overindulgence generates success. Curb your impulses. Adaptability and preparation for any possible change moves you through this cycle. Discipline, focus and commitment are the tools to achieve your goals.

PERSONAL YEAR

A year of transition and dynamic change; both planned and unexpected. A five year brings more change than any other. Be ready to take advantage of the many growth experiences possible now. This is a year of renaissance; let go of the challenges of the previous year and blaze a new trail. Liberty abounds now, compared to the restrictive four year. This is a good year to expand your horizons and take risks. Opportunities to find a new home, career, or new relationships are all available. Travel and adventure are at the forefront. Freedom and expansion reign, so be curious, reach new heights, and increase your peripheral vision. This is not the year to be timid, fearful, or overly cautious. Take advantage of freedom increasing opportunities, but with a modicum of balance. Beware of attracting too much drama or chaos. Make planned changes to improve your life; a new diet, exercise regime, or self-improvement course. Adapt to the fast pace and keep a positive attitude for a successful year. Luck is on your side. Change this year elevates your level of life and prepares you for the years to come.

PERSONAL MONTH

A month of unexpected change which brings travel and adventure. You may change directions entirely. Promote yourself and use your communication skills. Step up and take risks. The change in this month is for the betterment of life. Allow the energy to flow.

MISSING NUMBER

Without an E, N or W in your name, you may tend to be sheltered and shy away from crowds. You may fear change and prefer to live in your safe haven. One of your life lessons will be to learn constructive use of freedom and not squander opportunities. Have faith, take risks, and step out of your box. Adapt the vivacious five energy and explore the world. Let go of all fear and judgment of your past or future and live in the moment. Your greatest teacher is life experience. Broaden your visions and life experience. Learn to adapt to change and go with life's natural flow.

MULTIPLE NUMBER

If you have more than four fives in your name from the letters E, N, and W, you are a true freedom seeker. You are restless, active, and a curious risk taker who desires their personal freedom above all else. You like the avant-garde and prefer unique and unusual. You are a gifted communicator and languages come easy to you. You are prone to addictions and satisfying your senses with food, drug, alcohol, or sex is prevalent and problematic. Watch you don't overindulge. Your interests are varied which can make you a student of all trades, a master of none. You are impulsive and may quit too early or before you're complete. You desire your freedom because something better might come along. This is a future-oriented philosophy and prevents you from living in the present and making a commitment to the here and now.

PLANES OF EXPRESSION

Physical

You are the quintessential traveler. Your energy knows no bounds and your charisma attracts many people to you. You are versatile and adaptable. You prefer a life with limited restrictions so you can explore and expand your existence in your own avant-garde way.

Mental

You have a sharp mind and a quick wit. Knowledge comes easily to you when you're interested, especially anything new and unusual. You abhor the mundane and won't read the instruction manual. Decision making is challenging because you see both sides and want it all. You don't like deadlines or commitments. You are resourceful.

Emotional

You have the full range of emotions and have the ability to express all of them. You are quick to laugh or cry and have a fit of temper. Emotions don't run deep but rather come and go quickly. You don't hold onto them very long.

Intuitive

You have great flashes of intuition when you're open to them. You have the instinctual ability to know what to do next. With discipline and commitment, you can develop and expand your intuition to a deeper level.

NUMBER 5 SUMMARY

Your life will change. You can count on change wherever five appears. Expansion, freedom, adventure, and progressive growth. Your five senses come into play because you have a natural curiosity to touch, taste, smell, see and feel every exciting moment of life. You are the adventurer, the seeker of freedom who thrives on diversity. Your quick wit and charm are your gifts as is your adaptable flexibility. You desire to live life to the fullest and will stop at nothing to have a good time. Five is the number of senses, so pay attention to your addictions. Moderation is key as well as being grounded. You can fly higher when you have a stable launching platform.

A five year brings change in all forms. This is an expansive year and more life lessons appear this year than any other. Transition, transition, transition. Change will happen this year whether it is your address, your career, your personal growth, or any other aspect of your life. This is the year to take risks, unlike the previous four year when your nose is to the grindstone. Reach out, try new things, experience life to the fullest. This is your year to learn from every experience offered to you. Stay focused, don't get scattered, and don't create unnecessary drama.

Number 6

BALANCED: *Responsible, Service, Humanitarian, Cooperation, Love, Domesticity, Steady*

PASSIVE: *Worrisome, Meddling, Prideful, Unwilling To Serve, Co-dependent, Selfish, Heavily Burdened, Hypersensitive*

NEGATIVE: *Martyr, Self-Righteous, Emotionally Controlling, Passive-Aggressive, Cynical, Egotistical, Jealous*

CAREERS: *Caregiver, Healer, Counselor, Coach, Parent, Social Worker, Designer, Service Oriented Business*

LIFE PATH

Six is the number of love: romantic, caring, and benevolent. You are responsible, generous, kind, and have a sympathetic nature. Your life is about relationships, being of service with a foundation of love and beauty to support you. Success is achieved when you are helping others. Your love of humanity draws you into serving the greater good. You are a compassionate humanitarian, idealistic in your pursuit of truth and justice. Home and family are paramount, so be sure to balance your needs with others. You are a compassionate and nurturing parent and an understanding and supportive partner. Put on your oxygen mask first. If you give yourself the same amount of care you give others, your life will be fulfilled. A relationship ending in divorce is not a failure; it is an opportunity for you to learn more about relationships. Every relationship has its challenges and opportunities for personal growth. You appreciate luxury and express your artistic talents making your home beautiful. You have a fine character so don't waste your energy being controlling and demanding. Martyrdom does not suit you. You cannot please everyone all the time. Silence your inner critic and accept not everything is perfect. Respect the importance of boundaries. Your core desire to help others is commendable however you need to understand there is a difference between help and interference. Everyone has their own life lessons; you included. Ultimately, your life is about developing a relationship with yourself and being responsible for your own happiness and well-being. Love, appreciate and respect yourself.

DESTINY

Responsibility and service to your family and humanity rules your life. You are love in human expression and destined to share it joyfully. Nurturing and loving your family is job one. You service humanity through the love and beauty you bring to the world. You are the responsible caregiver and serve others, but it is important to remember to take care of yourself. It is imperative you balance the needs of others with your own. Maintaining a balanced exchange in relationships is paramount. You are an excellent partner and flourish in healthy relationships. You have a natural ability to be compassionate and understanding. You may know what is best for others, but it isn't always important to share it. You cannot fix everyone and it is important for you to understand everyone has their own challenges. There is a line between helping and interfering. Responsibility is a challenge when there is no love or beauty to support it. Your first responsibility is the relationship with yourself. Doing things because you want to do them is being responsible to yourself. Saying "no" is ok and can be an opportunity for personal growth. Your creative nature gives you an eye for beauty and you express it in the home. You are a genuinely loving and talented human being with the desire to be of service. Enjoy all of life's gifts and the finer things in life

SOUL

Your heart's desire is harmony in relationships and helping those you love. Six is the most loving and compassionate number. You are sympathetic, understanding, empathic, committed, and affectionate. Your love radiates outward in all directions; family, romantic relationships, nature, and humanity. You make an excellent spouse who thrives in a loving, committed relationship. Naturally supportive and nurturing, you desire to bring love and harmony to the world. Do not sacrifice yourself or your own personal needs. Remember to take care of yourself so you are able to give to others. You cannot take care of everyone, so be responsible to yourself first. Empower others by allowing them to learn their own life lessons. Self-empowerment comes when you focus on your own personal growth. We learn the most about ourselves in relationships. You have a deep appreciation for beauty and it is important you immerse yourself in it. Your love for the finer things in life are expressed in your home. Beauty feeds your soul, whether it is art you create or adventures in nature you experience.

PERSONALITY

Domestic life appeals to you. You are responsible and will take on more than is required of you for the sake of harmony. You are a compassionate counselor with a strong parental emphasis. You may sacrifice yourself for the good of others, but this can only go so far before it becomes a detriment to you. Playing the martyr is never comfortable or attractive. As a chosen confidant, friends and family turn to you for compassion, guidance, and support. You are an excellent committed spouse, but may have an idealistic view of romance. You cherish beauty and your artistic flair is expressed in your home. You dress with an eye for beauty, but won't sacrifice trends for comfort. You are a gifted teacher and counselor, ready to serve humanity.

MATURITY

Your concern for the welfare of others is paramount. You are a consummate giver and humanitarian. Your challenge is valuing your own time and not give too much of yourself to a cause. Heal yourself first and release any old resentments. You have an understanding of fairness and family values. You are a nurturer, counselor, and teacher; your family looks to you for support. You cannot fix everyone, however, and you would do well to understand there is a fine line between interfering and helping. Balance your needs with others lest you become a martyr or a zealot. You cherish beauty and love to express it in your home. A contented, happy home takes priority. Love yourself, create lasting and loving relationships and immerse yourself in beauty.

CURRENT NAME

The six vibration carries love, healing, nurturing, and a desire for service. You are a true friend who desires solid, lasting relationships. The six energy adds a touch of artistry to your life.

BIRTHDAY 6, 15, 24

You are a lover, teacher, nurturer and counselor. Relationships are everything and you are a true friend in every sense of the word. You love to be needed, but make sure you balance your needs with others. Understanding boundaries is a life lesson for the six and the earlier, the better. Compassion and generosity are in your wheelhouse and people turn to you for support. You don't always have to overdo everything.

MAJOR CYCLE

This major life cycle focuses on home and family. Responsibility at home and in all relationships are at the forefront. This is a time to make commitments, so marriage is likely. However, during this cycle, you need to review the status of previous commitments. If they cannot be met, divorce is possible. New opportunities to be of service arise and may test your entrepreneurial skills. Self-expression through any creative endeavor is encouraged now: dance, art, music, or any project to improve beauty in the home. Learn to balance other's needs with your own and understand codependency and martyrdom.

Formative

If your birthday is in June, your first major life cycle is a six. As a young person, you learn about relationships and what it means to be a member of a family. You tend toward the responsible side and may marry young. Relationships are paramount.

Progressive

If your birthday is 6, 15, or 24, your progressive cycle will focus on home, family, relationship, responsibility, and creativity. You'll likely marry and take on all domestic obligations. If during this time, your commitment breaks, you may seek divorce. Learning boundaries, balancing your needs with others are at the forefront. This is a highly creative time and usually focused on beautifying your home.

Wisdom

Family and a contented home fulfill your harvest years. You've learned to be the consummate nurturer and family look to you for support. You are a natural teacher and healer and able to serve your community with your many creative gifts. At this stage of your life you have developed many substantial and meaningful relationships.

PINNACLE

During this six pinnacle you will find your life focused on others. You may be overburdened with family responsibility or have many community obligations. This is the pinnacle to learn the importance of self-care and balance other's needs with those of your own. Setting personal boundaries while being of service to others defines this pinnacle. Responsibility is paramount, whether it is taking care of yourself or honoring your obligations. Being of service to others is revered more when honoring yourself in the process. Love is at the heart of this pinnacle and can mean growth in relationships. It is a growth period and you may be challenged when love is heightened in some romantic relationships. You now have the desire to help, but there is a difference between helping and meddling. Coming to the aid of others is where you shine, but establish clear boundaries and keep to them. If six is your first pinnacle, you may marry at a young age.

CHALLENGE

This is a time to learn responsibility, to yourself and to others. Your nurturing skills are required and you will learn healthy limits to responsible caregiving. Balance your needs with other's needs. Put your oxygen mask on first. Be your own best friend and do for yourself what you do for everyone else. Take on the gentle characteristics of the 6: loving, nurturing, and creating a welcoming home environment. Relationships teach us about ourselves and now is the time to develop a greater self-awareness. Shift your negative opinions and stubborn nature to the positive focus. Find gratitude for something in your life every day. Resist your meddlesome side and stick to your boundaries. Don't be a martyr and watch your urge toward codependence. You can be idealistic at times; don't always demand perfection. See the big picture and allow other perspectives to come into view. Learn to accept others the way they are.

ESSENCE

At the center of the six essence is love, home, family, and marriage. This is a time for responsibility to relationships, including yourself. Others see you as a support and a guiding light. Now is the time to be of service to support your family, friends, and community. Process unresolved issues as they surface. Improved business affairs and financial security are among the positive aspects of this essence. This is a progressive essence and a time for advancements in relationships, career, and finance. This is the time to balance your career with home and family. Your family may need you more than usual during this essence. Love is the core of number six and your relationships are tested during this essence. Your ability to express and receive love will be apparent. Lessons learned through relationships are paramount. Marriage, children, and expanding relationships are all possible. This is the marriage and divorce essence. Set your personal boundaries and end unhealthy relationships. Harmony as a driving force will reward your efforts. Strive for balance and your life will improve in this six essence. Your creative abilities expand.

PERSONAL YEAR

Home and family and relationships are at the forefront. Responsibility is paramount. This can be a challenging year because family needs you more than usual now. It is a time to express and receive love as it expands in a six year. Discover harmony in your relationships, health, and career. Forgiveness and letting go are always rewarded. You can reap the rewards of caregiving and being of service in this year. Take time to pass on your good ethics and values to children; nurture those you love — yourself included. Romance and other relationships are prevalent now. This is the year to renew your vows and take your relationship to a higher level. If the marriage is not your direction, this is the year to choose out of the commitment. It may take a few years to complete your decision. You may see progress in your career and finances. Career opportunities and community obligations come into view which may conflict with family and home. Now is the time to create harmony in all areas of your life. This is a year for movement forward in your own personal growth. Honor your responsibilities fully, but take care of yourself. Put your oxygen mask on first.

PERSONAL MONTH

This is your home and family month. Face your responsibilities and take care of your home and relationships. Use your time for family; schedule a vacation or work on home improvement projects. Find harmony in your career and at home. Realign your priorities.

MISSING NUMBER

If you do not have a F, O, or X in your name, you are prone to taking domestic life lightly. You may lack a sense of responsibility and duty and have difficulty committing to long term relationships. Embrace the characteristics of the six by being responsible to others. Understand your own needs and take care of yourself so you are able to take care of others. Learning to take responsibility and to love unconditionally — yourself included — will reward you with genuine long-lasting relationships.

MULTIPLE NUMBER

If you have one or two 6's in your name from F, O, or X, you clearly know right from wrong. You are a confident parent and gifted nurturer. You shine when you are in service to humanity. Many 6's in your name signify you have strong family values, but may take responsibility for everyone and everything. Don't sacrifice yourself for others, you do not need to be a martyr. You are fiercely loyal and demand the same in return. Define your boundaries and stick to them. Your opinions matter to you and you many of them.

PLANES OF EXPRESSION

Physical

Home and family are your focus. You are cultured. You have good taste and this is expressed in your home. Relationships are important to you and you respond well to approval and appreciation. You balance romance with practicality and make a good mate. Remember to take care of yourself so you are able to aid others.

Mental

You are dependable and reliable and react efficiently in an emergency situation. You are a creative artist who can teach as well. You care deeply for others and have healing abilities.

Emotional

You are the best friend and partner. You are kind, romantic, empathetic, loyal, and nurturing. You are a consummate giver and may have a difficult time with boundaries. You tend to worry and care too much about the judgments of others.

Intuitive

You tend to be so outwardly focused on the needs of others that you pay little attention to your own intuition. However, you are highly intuitive and spiritual. You may have insights about friends and family and should take them seriously.

NUMBER 6 SUMMARY

Relationships are paramount, and when a six appears, it is time to pay attention to them. A six in your chart signifies the consummate caregiver and nurturer. You are one who loves home and family and expresses your inner beauty throughout your environment. You are kind hearted, care deeply for others and too often put their needs ahead of your own. You take your responsibilities seriously, preferring to always do the "right" thing and feel guilty when you believe you could have done more. Loving devotion and being of service to those you love is your greatest joy, but remember to value yourself in the process. Counseling, teaching, healing, and caregiving are all noble pursuits.

A six year brings a magnifying glass to all relationships. This is the divorce or marriage year and everything in between. You may renew your vows or choose another direction. This is the time to deal with relationship issues because they will come to the forefront now. If you're single, a new romance is on the horizon. You will find harmony in finances and your career as new opportunities arise. Find time to service a valuable cause which brings you joy. Heal your resentments, find new ways to love and honor yourself. Be responsible and discover new ways to relish beauty everywhere.

Number 7

BALANCED: *Analytical, Seeker, Spiritual, Technical Abilities, Researcher, Intuitive, Mystical, Metaphysical. Faith, Trust*

PASSIVE: *Skeptical, Cynical, Withdrawn, Secretive, Inferiority Complex, Aloof, Erratic*

NEGATIVE: *Deceitful, Sneaky, Critical, Intellectually Conceited, Eccentric, Vain*

CAREERS: *Technology, Psychology, Science, Lawyer, Judge, Research, Spiritualist*

LIFE PATH

You are a born seeker. The search for wisdom and understanding of all things fuels your life. You ask the big questions; Who am I? Why am I here? You have strong analytical skills, a high intellect, and accept nothing at face value. Seven is the metaphysical number and you are a seeker of the truth in all things. You are the observer, researcher and skeptic who abhors a crowd. Philosophical in your approach to life, you spend much of your time in quiet contemplation. Technology is natural for you and is a field in which you are likely to excel. Metaphysical interests direct you on your spiritual path to solving the mysteries of life. Your life lesson is to connect to your spiritual guidance and have the faith to follow it. You need your space and privacy. You may enjoy being the center of attention, but require solitude for balance. You are a private person and intimacy can be a challenge for you which can cause you to feel lonely at times.

You can be overly critical or skeptical and spend too much energy on thinking through every little detail. Sarcasm and cynicism make up your negative side. You may not always be forthcoming and tend to omit valid information. Your rejuvenation time is best spent inwardly focused on walks in nature. You may be a recluse who, when rejected, feels sorry for yourself. You are frequently misunderstood because you retreat to your safe place, rather than face a conflict to clear the air. Be careful not to become too withdrawn and independent. This may push others away and you will not experience true friendship or intimacy. This is a lifetime learning great lessons as you ponder the deeper meaning of life. And, reward comes when you share your wisdom with humanity.

DESTINY

Your destiny is to analyze, contemplate, and deconstruct all you learn. You have keen research and observation skills. Your life is dedicated not only to the pursuit of wisdom and truth, but with sharing your knowledge as well. You have a strong interest in science, philosophy, and metaphysics. You possess the ability to see different perspectives and may get bogged down in the details. You dislike anything superficial and uninteresting. You are not a social person and prefer your own company spent in solitude. You can be in the limelight, but need quiet time to bring life into balance. You have a strong analytical and logical mind. You make a keen researcher, analyst, lawyer, or philosopher. Create a relationship with your higher guidance and trust it. Have faith to follow your Divine path and share the wisdom with the world. You are a private person and can be seen as aloof and a loner. Too much solitude can distance you from others and cause you to be critical and cynical. Your darker side lacks integrity and when in charge, may cause you to be dishonest and unfaithful. This is your life's mission. Skepticism, cynicism and perfectionism are your weaknesses. Don't let these stop you from sharing all you know and imparting your wisdom is your destiny. You require alone time daily for inner reflection. This is a great benefit not only to you, but to others around you.

SOUL

You keep your emotions close to your chest and prefer solitude to partnership. Marriage isn't for you unless your partner also has seven energy in their chart and understands your need for your alone time. You are highly perceptive and are driven to know all the mysteries of the universe. You are a perfectionist and can be overly critical at times, focusing on what is wrong rather than appreciation of all that is right. You have space in your heart for the Divine and you would do well to discover your faith sooner rather than later. Asking life's big questions helps you find your spiritual path. Listening and trusting your inner guidance will serve you greatly in this life. You are a sensitive soul and require a substantial amount of time in contemplation. Your intimacy is best enjoyed in nature. Your analytical heart prefers discussions to include the business side of relationships and not the emotional side. You see the black and white in thoughts, but emotions are nebulous and unnecessary. The heart is unpredictable, and so, you don't trust feelings. It is a growth experience for you to be in a relationship where you trust someone with your heart. Searching for greater wisdom is your heart's desire and when you share all you learn is when your soul is fulfilled.

PERSONALITY

People see you as reserved, aloof, mysterious, and intelligent; a philosopher of sorts. You are introspective and introverted and your tastes may tend toward the unconventional. You are prone to withdraw into yourself and are frequently unavailable, so friendships can be difficult to maintain. You can appear negative, skeptical, and cynical. You are seen as an intellectual and respected, but guard against thinking you know it all and have it all figured out. You prefer only to discuss what interests you and when talking about those things, you are a gifted speaker and teacher. You need your quiet time for contemplation and regeneration. Trust in your friends and allow them to see your mystical side. Share all the knowledge you gain and teach others. You will all benefit.

MATURITY

Your middle years bring a sense of peace and tranquility. You are here to study life's mysteries and understand it is sacred. Your analytical skills are masterful. You are serious and a seeker of philosophical truths. Metaphysics and science bring out those seeker qualities. Solitude is your friend and you find a lot of time spent in quiet contemplation. Your intuition grows stronger as you age as you delve deeper into your studies. An escape into nature is where you feel at home. You enjoy living uniquely to fully explore your thoughts. However, too much alone time isn't good for you. Watch you don't become withdrawn or begin to feel sorry for yourself. Following your intuition will always reward you with answers. You are mature enough to go deeper within to search for wisdom and understanding. Your time is well spent reading, contemplation, and solitary walks in nature to pursue spiritual insights. Meditation is always a benefit to you.

CURRENT NAME

The seven energy adds study and research to your many talents. You may need more solitude as you contemplate metaphysics, philosophy, or technology. Develop your intuition. Trust may be an issue in relationships.

BIRTHDAY 7, 16, 25

As a 7 birthday, you are a gifted intuitive with exceptional psychic abilities. Study and research, technology, and science are worthwhile pursuits. You are best served when you spend quality solitude time in nature. Rejuvenation and regeneration are healthy rewards for your physical and spiritual self.

MAJOR CYCLE

A spiritual cycle will take you to a deeper understanding. Study, research, investigate, and gain skills to improve yourself. This is time for contemplation and a spiritual quest. Your intuition is enhanced and a good time to go inward to develop wisdom. Your hermitage cycle means relationships take a back seat now, so understanding is required. All of this introspection brings forth wisdom which is to be shared through teaching, counseling, or writing. It is an opportune time to study science, technology, or metaphysics during this cycle.

Formative

If you have a July birthday, number seven rules your first life cycle. You are wise beyond your years and ask the big life questions at a young age. What is the meaning of life? Why am I here? How does it all work? You may feel you don't belong at times but find you prefer spending time alone anyway. This is the cycle to follow your passions and discover your chosen field.

Progressive

If your birthday falls on 7, 16, or 25, seven rules your second life cycle. Seven is the number of metaphysics, philosophy, science, psychology, and technology. This 29 year era is the time to study, enhance your skills and expand your knowledge. You have the ability to become an authority in your field. Teaching and passing on your wisdom are as important as learning it. Time alone is necessary for introspection and rejuvenation. It is wise to choose a partner who understands and supports your alone time. A spiritual path and meditation are positive pursuits to enhance this cycle.

Wisdom

The harvest cycle brings spiritual development. Introspection, study and gaining knowledge are at the forefront. Prayer and meditation enhance your wisdom and your intuition fuels your daily life. Meditative health practices, such as yoga or Tai Chi keep you healthy and focused. Pursuing life's big questions is what you want to ponder through metaphysics, science, and technology. Serving humanity by teaching all you learned is rewarded. You are an authority and people look to you for guidance.

PINNACLE

A seven pinnacle signifies the time you search for the meaning of life. You often feel alone and "I want to do it alone," is your mantra. You are introspective, contemplative, and walk the spiritual path. Solving life's big questions is paramount now. Science and technology come easy to you and now is a good time for research and study. Make time for introspection and developing your spiritual side. Your critical voice is louder now as you seek perfection in all things. Acknowledge what is right as well as what is flawed. There is perfection in imperfection. During later pinnacle cycles, you have the opportunity to hone your skills and delve deeper inward. Time in nature is the best environment for rest and rejuvenation. A seven pinnacle cycle can be challenging to a relationship because of the necessary solitude you seek. This can be a time of the "dark night of the soul," which can be daunting. However, this is for your inner development and spiritual growth. You emerge more knowledgeable and content in your understanding of life's mysteries. This pinnacle offers the opportunity for deep insights and great understanding. Gaining wisdom and teaching what you know energizes this pinnacle.

CHALLENGE

The seven energy brings isolation and solitude. Inward focus on your personal development and awakening your spirit will bring rewards in this serious cycle. Learn to have faith in yourself and your inner guidance. Follow your inner voice as your intuition increases. Find peace and contentment within, and you will be able to create a relationship with the Divine. Build relationships you can trust. Be your genuine self and connect with others. Use your alone time wisely to ponder the mysteries of life. Now is the time to develop your spiritual path and follow it. Meditate. Contemplate the metaphysical. This is the time for inward focus and study. Being alone is part of the challenge, but don't completely isolate yourself from others. This is a spiritual quest and one which feeds your soul. Trust is the bottom line for a successful seven challenge. Have faith in your intuition, your inner guidance, and know the Universe works. You may have to stand on the precipice to take a leap of faith.

ESSENCE

Now is the time for solitude and introspection. Explore higher dimensions, be open to psychic experiences, and ponder life's big questions. Your energy is best spent focused on yourself for inner growth. Your intuition is elevated and you are more sensitive than normal. Follow the advice of your inner guidance. Your focus and keen thought process are heightened. Committing to a spiritual quest to understand the meaning of life is a worthwhile pursuit in a seven essence. Choose a specific field in which to specialize. Investigate, study, and research for a rewarding cycle. This can be a time of separation or loss for the purpose of spiritual growth. Your inward focus creates the possibility of a spiritual awakening now. Study metaphysics and other alternative teachings. Spend time in nature, meditate, and watch your health.

PERSONAL YEAR

Now is the time to focus inward after a six year of service and family. You need solitude, rest, and time to reexamine your life's directions. This seven vibration brings spiritual pursuits and studying life's mysteries. Now is a good time to undertake a vision quest or take self-improvement classes. Take care of yourself and research new health regimes. This is the year for introspection, developing your intuition, and achieving your inner peace. Your internal self takes precedence now and may cause challenges to a relationship. Time spent focused on self-improvement will ultimately improve your daily life. Now is the time to study science, technology, or metaphysics. Develop a healthy regime that focuses on your physical, mental, and spiritual sides. Trust your intuition and have the faith to follow it. This is the year for following your guidance. You are strengthening the foundation of your inner self. A year spent on self-awareness and personal growth is rewarded in the following years. Rest and attend to your health, this year more than others. Seven is the number of legal issues so be aware.

PERSONAL MONTH

Rest. Relaxation. Rejuvenation. Solitude is necessary for inward focus. Reevaluate where your life has been and the direction you are going. Study metaphysics. Take a retreat. Spend time in nature.

MISSING NUMBER

If you do not have a G, P, or Y in your name, you will need to discover your spiritual side. Uncover your inner truth. Trust is your issue and learning to trust your intuition, spiritual guidance, and your higher power will have great benefits. Have faith in others and in the power of love. Trust in the Universe. Not all is learned or taught on the physical plane.

MULTIPLE NUMBER

If you have one or two sevens in your name from G, P, or Y, you have a highly developed intuition. Your interests are spiritually focused at home and in the world of metaphysics. Researcher, teacher, inventor, computer wizard. Three or more sevens and your gifts lie in the analytical realm. You want to understand and intuitively do most situations. Technology, research and metaphysics are your interests. You have an unusual need for your alone time and prefer time spent in meditation or contemplation. You care for others, but are not demonstrative. You're likely aloof and can be seen as eccentric.

PLANES OF EXPRESSION

Physical

You prefer your alone time and you need it for rejuvenation and regeneration. You have a few selective friends who have passed your personal test and are now trustworthy. You prefer philosophical discussions over social media chatter. You are reserved and can appear aloof. You may have health challenges and will do well to take care of your body. Good nutrition and holistic methods of healing.

Mental

You are a brilliant thinker who loves to analyze everything. You are observant, introspective, and tend to take life seriously. You love knowledge and learning and make an excellent scholar. You delve deep into your studies; preferring not to waste time on the superficial. You tend to be overly critical because of your intense desire to get to the bottom of things. Looking at the positive side will serve you more than finding fault with everything. Learn to trust and have faith in the Divine.

Emotional

You appear to have few emotions, preferring to keep your feelings to yourself. You can appear aloof and are undemonstrative. You can be hurt however and have fits of melancholy if you allow your feelings to build up inside. Feeling sorry for yourself serves no one and you will do well to allow your emotions to flow spontaneously.

Intuitive

You are naturally intuitive and have great inner wisdom. You have sparks of intuition and incredible insights. Metaphysics comes naturally to you and having an understanding of this science will be of great benefit in expanding your inner wisdom.

NUMBER 7 SUMMARY

Analyst, Truth Seeker, Mystic, Philosopher, Investigator. You require your own private time for inner reflection and rejuvenation. You ask the big questions and seriously want to know the answers. You are excellent with technology and research; studying and reading are your strengths. You require a spiritual path for inner reflection and guidance; metaphysics come naturally to you. You prefer being alone with your own thoughts to a social gathering. You are a skeptic and take little at face value, preferring to test and analyze. All partners should understand your need for solitude; anyone who expects otherwise will be disappointed. Watch you aren't too cynical or critical and hold your perfectionism to a moderate degree. Emerge from your solitude once in a while and be a member of the modern world.

A seven year is slower and offers you much time for inner reflection. This is the year to go inward and ask your questions: Where is my life going? What is my purpose? The answers may change the course of your life. Take a soul retreat or a vision quest to improve yourself. The seven energy supports your spiritual journey and this is the time to enhance your spiritual connection and create a solid inner foundation. Have a psychic reading, study metaphysics, be open to where your spiritual path leads you — especially this year. Sit in quiet introspection and reexamine your life. This is the year for a reset, not only spiritually, but physically and mentally as well. Detox, body cleanse, pay attention to your health.

Number 8

BALANCED: *Authority, Successful, Natural Executive, Honors Wealth, Confident, Considerate Manager, Prosperous, Discriminating, Personal Mastery*

PASSIVE: *Fears Failure, Refuses to Lead, Disrespectful, Careless with Money, Demands Recognition, Compulsive, Obsessive*

NEGATIVE: *Excessive Ambition, Power Hungry, Egocentric, Abusive, Materialistic, Revengeful, Unscrupulous*

CAREERS: *Manager, Executive, Entrepreneur, Lawyer, Judge*

LIFE PATH

The number eight characteristics are: power, authority, ambition, leadership, wealth, prosperity, excellence, success, balance, harmony. A natural manager who attracts abundance. Strong problem-solving skills and a head for business. Driven with a potential of self-mastery. Expands the visions of seven energy toward the humanitarian service of the nine.

You are a natural born business executive who exudes power and authority. Self-improvement defines your success and you are given tools to achieve mastery. Eight energy is demanding and requires you to strive to be the best version of yourself.

You are a visionary. Take charge and exercise your entrepreneurial skills because people see you as an authority and respect your superior judgment. You are here to understand the value of money and the quality of life. You are either good with money naturally, or struggle with it. You may create more than one fortune, having lost some along the way. Life will provide the necessary experiences for you to fully understand the value of money. If your fortune is built on a faulty foundation of greed, deception, and negativity, it will likely disappear. You learn resilience and have the ability to recover from failure. Eight is the number for stability and it is required in all facets of life. Keep your equilibrium. Find harmony with your career and your family life even though you may want to be at the office more. This is your lifetime to balance your spiritual world with your material world. Living with integrity and honesty is rewarded as is a positive mindset. What you put out will return to you, "as above, so below." You reap what you sow.

DESTINY

Eight is the number of self-mastery and you are destined to reclaim your power to achieve success. Achievement in business management and organization are your driving forces and you have the potential for great success in your chosen field. You are an excellent judge of character and have a strong intuition in business endeavors. You make a demanding leader but don't ask more from someone than you ask of yourself. You have the ability to become the authority and people look to you for guidance. You are a born leader and authority; put your skills to good use in any business endeavor. You may let your ego rule you or allow spiritual guidance to direct you. You will have many opportunities to choose either the light or the dark path. Either way, your destiny is to know your own genuine power. What goes around, comes around, so be aware of what you send out because you'll get it back. Setting clear goals and having a vision pave your road to success. Believe in your high ideals, keep a positive mindset to manifest abundance. Remember happiness doesn't come from money alone. Eight is the balance number so it is imperative you learn to balance material and spiritual worlds. Watch your tenacity and overambitious nature don't get the best of you. Temper your tendencies to be stubborn and impatient.

SOUL

Being a visionary and managing others to achieve your goals is your heart's desire. And, you desire to be a success in everything you endeavor to do. You are a visionary and your talents lie in creating a team to manifest your dreams. Balance, harmony, and power are the energies feeding your soul. You're all business in career, home, and relationships. Power, money and self-importance color your idea of romance. You prefer partners who equal your business acumen. Remember to temper your need to be right all the time. Looking for the win-win solution will serve you best. It is important for you to always have a project; something towards which you direct your energy. Challenges in your life teach you the skills you will need to achieve the many goals you have set for yourself. Have the courage to face your fears, follow a strong moral compass and you will succeed.

PERSONALITY

People see you as powerful, ambitious, and influential. You have an impressive and influential presence which others see as an authority. You emanate an air of confidence and sound judgment. Others look to you for your leadership judgment. You have a business mind and are an exemplary manager. Looking the part as an executive and dressing for success is important to you. You are a visionary and your organizational skills aid your achievements. Understanding how to manage and delegate, not control and micromanage are keys to your success. Keep your ego in check. Do not be greedy or merciless. Serving the greater good brings greater rewards. Positive ethics and a strong moral code are imperative.

MATURITY

You may see your career and commitment to success expand now. You have the energy behind you to become an expert in your field. You will likely not retire, having the drive to always be doing something. The eight on its side signifies infinity and is the quintessential symbol for balance. Having your material and spiritual worlds in harmony aid your achievements. Your management and organizational skills along with your strong intellect give you a sturdy foundation for success. Your drive to succeed is worthy, however save time for humanitarian efforts. You can achieve a high level of self-mastery which inspires others to see you as an authority. Serving humanity will get you further than just serving your own needs. Be open to guidance from a higher power, adopt good ethics and abundance flows to you. If greed and fame rule, your success can dissipate. You reap what you sow. Achieve self-mastery.

CURRENT NAME

Adds achievement, leadership and attracts abundance. Gives you the ability to understand money and business. Maintaining a positive attitude and having a strong moral code create a foundation on which to build a successful career. Self-mastery is your goal.

BIRTHDAY 8, 17, 26

As an eight birthday, you have strong organization and management skills. You have a knack for leadership and others look to you for guidance. You have the potential for great material wealth, but remember to help humanity and not just yourself. Money isn't everything and rewards come when you serve the greater good.

MAJOR CYCLE

Money and recognition rule this cycle. Focus on hard work toward a suitable career and you'll see financial rewards. Learning from mistakes and problem solving are key here. You learn management and organizational skills as the big picture comes into view. You are compelled to succeed and your drive to achieve is greater now. You are seen as an authority in your later years. Balance and harmony energize the eight.

Formative

If you are born in August, eight rules your formative cycle. You learn the value of financial stability at a young age-possibly through the lack of it. During this stage you develop a moral code with regard to money and power.

Progressive

If your birthday is on 8, 17, or 26, number eight rules your progressive cycle. You learn to have a positive relationship with money through diligent work and honorable ethics. This can be a time for reversal of fortune if you are prone to greed or illegal activity. You reap what you sow. Focus on the positive, serve the greater good and abundance flows to you. Understanding success in life is not just defined by wealth and status.

Wisdom

Your harvest years produce wealth and rewards provided you have an attitude of abundance. You are seen as an authority figure and will continue to work until you are unable. A level of self-mastery is attainable if you embrace a strong moral code. You need to try to serve the greater good and not just yourself to bring substantial rewards. Your senior years are financially secure if you understand the ebb and flow of eight energy. Inheritance is possible and you are likely not to retire.

PINNACLE

You learn the value of authority and may challenge the powers that be. You establish your own personal power and it is increased under this pinnacle. You will learn what it means to be an authority. Eight pinnacle is learning self-mastery and authenticity. Your judgment is tested as you have opportunities to develop your management and organizational skills. Have the courage to take on large projects, the energy is with you. Honesty and integrity are required for a successful pinnacle. Desire is for achievement in the business world; home and family are secondary in this pinnacle. Developing your own personal power and how to serve humanity for the good of all. A positive point of view and an attitude of abundance are continually rewarded. Careful money management sets a strong foundation for a financially secure future. Harmony and balance are required for true self-mastery. Balance your career and your home life as well as your material and spiritual worlds. This pinnacle is an opportunity to learn the value of money. It may flow easily to you and you manage it well, or you may have serious money concerns until you learn the lesson. Money is not the only measure of success and bringing balance to all aspects of your life will serve you best.

CHALLENGE

Eight challenge energy focuses on money, achievement, and material issues. Balancing your life on all levels is important now. Follow the golden rule now more than ever. What you put out now will return to you in spades. Understanding money and materialism are not the keys to a fulfilled life. Authenticity, a good moral code, and integrity build a solid foundation for success. Reclaim your personal power, step up and achieve your goals. Embrace the Universal Law of Abundance and allow the natural flow of energy to you. Do not focus all your time and energy on making money. Selfish greed only serves instant gratification. Rewards come when you serve the greater good. You may have money now, but it can dissipate just as quickly. You reap what you sow. This challenge gives you the opportunity to see there is more to life than material wealth. This is a spiritual challenge which brings to the forefront your weaknesses. You will learn where your energy is best directed to achieve the greatest success. Balancing your material and spiritual worlds is key to mastering this challenge.

ESSENCE

Balance and harmony rule the eight essence. This is a time of expansion and personal progress. Business is the driving force; take advantage of opportunities for expansion and advancement. There may be many. You will likely make money, but be sure to protect it. This is the time you will use your sharp business acumen. Develop a positive attitude of abundance. Know what true giving and receiving means. Balance your material and spiritual realms. Bring harmony to your work and rejuvenation time. Stand with a valid moral code and strong work ethics to realize your dreams. You may be required to defend your personal power to learn a valuable life lesson.

PERSONAL YEAR

The eight year focuses on discovering your personal power and dealing with authority issues. Many life lessons come into view in this physical year. Focus on your career and expand your career, the eight energy is behind you. A management position may open up where you are the authority. Take the lead now and step into your own power. This is an expansive, empowerment cycle to learn to be the authority. You are more powerful now and your mental capabilities are stronger than usual. Be more focused and follow your intuition. Have the courage to face your fears and step outside the box. This is the year to take risks. Confrontation with those who previously disempowered you is possible. Money is at the center and flows heavily this year. You will see rewards after your diligent efforts of the earlier years. Watch your spending and focus on the greater for a profitable year. Manifest your dreams by integrating your material and spiritual worlds. Wealth is not the only measure of success. You get back what you put out, so keep a positive attitude and serve the greater good, not your ego. Greater rewards come when you embrace strong morals and ethics. Life is more than your financial report. If you only focus on money, your life is about money. Money is energy and it ebbs and flows. If you focus on only increasing your bank balance then that's all you have. If you just serve your own selfish pursuits, your money can disappear. Serving the greater good ensures a lasting relationship with wealth.

PERSONAL MONTH

Eight is a working month with emphasis on power and authority. Business is the focus, and you are required to take the leadership role. Organize and manage all aspects of your life. Balance your material and spiritual worlds. Be the authority.

MISSING NUMBER:

Without an H, Q, or Z in your name, you will have life lessons concerning money and power. Learning to balance material and spiritual worlds also comes into your realm. Reclaim your power and understand the Law of Attraction. You have a resistance to authority figures and it is important that you learn to temper your power with respect. Leadership alongside others, not controlling them is key. Understand that money doesn't define you. Embrace honorable ethics to develop a fine moral character.

MULTIPLE NUMBER

If you have an H, Q, or Z in your name, you are gifted with strong management and organizational skills. More than one eight signifies you are a diligent worker driven to succeed. You are goal oriented and a visionary which are the foundations for your success. You see others for who they are and recognize their strengths and weaknesses. Your focus is on seriously making money, but be alert to ego and greedy tendencies. There is more to life than money. A wise direction is to discover harmony in material and spiritual worlds. Achieving self-mastery is possible.

PLANES OF EXPRESSION

Physical

You have a strong drive, unlimited energy, and a powerful inner strength. You are loyal and devoted, but tend to dominate because of your powerful character. You prefer the grand version of life and never settle for the typical or mediocre. Your competitive nature encourages you to reach great heights where you are innately comfortable. You are a consummate manager and builder, ambitious to the core. You enjoy exhibiting your success and great wealth. You work more than rest and your challenge is to balance material and spiritual worlds.

Mental

You are an authority and have excellent judgment and management skills. You can follow the letter of the law, or may choose just the opposite. Your ambition and competitive nature are your foundation for success. You are an authority and command respect. Watch your feelings of superiority and self-importance. You are highly demanding of others and yourself. You refuse to settle for less.

Emotional

You prefer to be in charge due to your strong character and desire to dominate. You have a passionate nature and are concerned for issues close to your heart. You may have fits of anger and are not comfortable with others' feelings. You are an impartial judge, honest and fair. You don't show your intimate feelings; you're all business, but you do have a sentimental, romantic side when you allow it to appear.

Intuitive

Your advanced management skills and strong business acumen is where your intuition resides. You have keen perception abilities which make you an excellent judge of character. Your intuition is powerful in the business and management realm.

NUMBER 8 SUMMARY

Business Manager, Organizer, Leader, Financier, Authority. You are a master organizer and able to run any business. An eight in your chart signifies lessons with money, so you are excellent with money or you are the exact opposite. You will have the opportunity to learn how to manifest your dreams. Eight is the number of self-mastery and life offers lessons of your own power and authority. Eight is the karmic balance number and carries the vibration, "reap what you sow." Harmony and balance flow through every aspect of your lifetime. All will come to you if you focus on the positive, adopt an attitude of abundance, and have high moral standards.

An eight year is a busy, outward focused year. This is the time to get organized, plan for the future and manifest your dreams. You learn about your own personal power, deal with authority issues and may be thrust in a leadership role. A year to test your mettle and stand up for yourself. Make sure you aren't spending all your time at work. This year will give you an opportunity to balance your time at work and home. This is a karmic balance year so you'll get back what you put out in the Universe. Keep a steady moral compass, focus on the greater good and rewards will find you. Greed and ego centered pursuits will bite you in the behind.

Number 9

BALANCED: *Universal Love, Selfless Service, Karmic Law, Philanthropic, Divine Energy in Everything, Compassion, Artistic, Humanitarian*

PASSIVE: *Aimless, Gullible, Indifferent, Depressed, Pessimistic, Indiscreet, Impractical*

NEGATIVE: *Bitter, Ill-Tempered, Unethical, Disregards Resources*

CAREERS: *Artist, Teacher, Doctor, Writer, Actor, Philosopher, any Service Industry*

LIFE PATH

Your life path leads to an understanding of interconnectedness of all things. This is the path of Universal Love and compassion. The world's problems concern you deeply and you believe you know the solutions. You live by a strict moral code and have elevated ideals. You follow the golden rule: "Do unto others," and don't understand why others do not. The underlined energy in all your endeavors is to uplift humanity. You are a compassionate humanitarian. Temper your perfectionism and work on acceptance. Rise above the melodrama in your life and then you can set to work making it a better place. Releasing your judgments and learning forgiveness improves your life path. You honor Universal Love and believe there is Divine energy in all things. Your appreciation for creativity in life is at the highest levels and you strive to raise the Universal Consciousness to love all that is. Forgiveness, compassion, acceptance, and unconditional love are your driving forces. You understand there is a connectedness to everything. Nine is the number of completion and therefore events, relationships, experiences, projects and all elements of your life may come to a conclusion. You are an old soul completing tasks from many lifetimes. You are here to be of service to all humanity and make the world a better place. This is Universal-God energy and you have a desire to fully comprehend it. Learn to forgive, love unconditionally, and accept yourself and others just as you are. Numbers three, six, and nine all represent different aspects of love, creativity, and service. The characteristics of nine are: Universal Love. Altruism, Compassion. Benevolence. Creative Artist. Unconditional Love. Seeker of Universal Harmony. Aimless at times, gullible or feel powerless. Generous to a fault. Idealistic, indiscreet, pessimistic. Intolerant, unforgiving and temperamental.

DESTINY

You endeavor to bring humanity together using unconditional love and selflessness. You are destined to make the world a better place through unconditional love and forgiveness. You are a true humanitarian in every sense of the word. Divine Love is your vibration and you're destined to share it. A traveler at heart, you adventure to many other walks of life. Nine is the number of completion and you are here to bring to a close previously uncompleted life lessons. Your life experience will run the gamut of all the numbers to learn what it means to be human. You will experience heartbreak and loss as well as euphoric joy. The result of these intense life lessons is a higher awareness of the beauty in life. "Let go and let God" is your mantra. You understand forgiveness is paramount to move you toward your destiny for transformation and healing. You stand for everything fine and beautiful in the world. Surrender your judgments and accept everyone has their own life lessons. Honor and respect their boundaries as well as create some of your own. Love for all of humanity is the foundation to achieve your destiny.

SOUL

The most compassionate of hearts wishes to love the world and everything in it. You are idealistic to the core. Having life lessons focused on loss, nine souls have the biggest hearts. Your love is your most valuable asset and generated outward makes you an influential humanitarian. Beauty and love fuel your heart's desire. Divine intuition comes naturally to you to create a loving nature. Your boundless love and creative energy fuel your desire to serve humanity. You are here to love and forgive yourself to the highest degree. When you align your infinite Divine Love with your creative energy and focus on the greater good, you fulfill your heart's desire.

PERSONALITY

You are seen as a compassionate and generous humanitarian. Emotionally sensitive, and highly intuitive, you can be philosophical. You have a wise worldly view and are intolerant of injustice. Idealistic and gullible at times, but sympathetic and understanding. Humility, tolerance, and patience are qualities to develop. Learn to adapt.

MATURITY

It is a spiritual world for you, not a material one; a life of service, not personal gain. You see a beautiful life is filled with peace, love, and joy. You have had to let go in your life because nine is the number for loss. Your material life is surrendered for a spiritual one. You let go of judging others for a deeper love of humanity. You are a true humanitarian, compassionate to the core. You are a lightworker for Universal Love and Compassion. Use your creative artistic abilities to help your community and environment. Tolerance can get you so far, but detachment brings in a higher vibration. Use your energy for unconditional love, acceptance and forgiveness.

CURRENT NAME

Expands your creative abilities and encourages compassion for humanity. Serve the greater good by being unconditionally loving. Tolerate and accept others. Donate your time for community causes. Forgiveness will always serve you.

BIRTHDAY 9, 18, 27

You are compassionate, tolerant, and understanding. You are creative, generous, and idealistic to a fault sometimes. Learn forgiveness and let go of injustices; it will serve you throughout your lifetime. Focus on unconditional love, not vengeance.

MAJOR CYCLES

Selfless service to humanity fuels this cycle. Let go, forgive, and move on to making the world a better place. Universal compassion is key as you develop a concern for the welfare of others. The lesson of this cycle is: We are all connected. It is time to enhance your intuition and spiritual growth. Your rewards come when you live a selfless and service-driven life. See the greater good and move toward a time of humanitarian service.

Formative

If you were born in September, you learned compassion at a young age. Lessons emerge to teach forgiveness and compassion toward humanity. Seeing the bigger picture and helping others are at the forefront. Your creativity is enhanced and encouraged.

Progressive

If your birthday falls on 9, 18, or 27, you will have many opportunities to learn compassion and forgiveness in this progressive cycle. Discover new worlds, study different cultures, and uncover the bigger picture of humanity. All life lessons direct you to a cause for serving humanity, whether it be environmental or community based. These years can change your life and offer you an opportunity to serve the greater good. Creativity is heightened, so find an outlet for your talents. Do not waste this transformational period in your life.

Wisdom

Contentment and peace fulfill your wisdom years provided you've learned to let go and forgive. Now is the time to give back the knowledge you have accumulated over the years and be of service to humanity. Teaching and donating your energy selflessly is rewarded. Explore and use your creative efforts for the betterment of mankind.

PINNACLE

Number 9 for a first pinnacle always means you are an old soul and have wisdom beyond your years. There is usually early loss in life with a 9 first pinnacle. Lessons come through loss and suffering. This can be a challenging time as nine is the number of endings. You also have infinite potential for greatness. You are compassionate and sensitive and now is the time to demonstrate your understanding and empathy. Forgiveness and acceptance begins with you. As an old soul, you know there is more to life than pain and suffering. You have a larger view of life and at times feel life is bigger than you are. You desire to make the world a better place and might struggle with the perfect career. Find ways to keep yourself grounded, lest you get lost in cosmic consciousness. Tolerance, forgiveness and compassion are key for a successful pinnacle. Learn Universal principles and adhere to the Golden Rule and rewards abound. Don't try to fix everyone, allow them their own personal growth lessons. Your service is in accepting who they are and loving them unconditionally. Focus on the beauty and harmony in the world and bring joy and understanding wherever you go. Sidestep the drama and instead focus on unconditionally humanity.

0 CHALLENGE

There is no 9 challenge.

A 0 Challenge can be a period of tremendous growth. You are free to choose to deal with all of the number challenges or with none of them. If you choose not to take on a challenge, you are free to drift along in life. If you desire to reach your greatest potential and achieve a higher level of understanding, then you will have many challenging life experiences. You may feel the challenge vibration of every number in your life at the same moment. This can be an intense era with a lot of changes. It carries with it multiple opportunities for considerable personal growth. Your best success during this period is to have an understanding of all the vibrations: Number 1 is independence; 2 is diplomacy; 3 is positivity; 4 is structure; 5 is adaptability; 6 is responsibility; 7 is wisdom; 8 is mastery and 9 is service. Have gratitude for life and take time for regeneration. The possibilities are limitless if you choose to make the world a better place and serve the greater good. This is a sign of an old soul.

ESSENCE

This is a time when Universal Love and forgiveness reign supreme. You may have many experiences which result in spiritual expansion. Your intuition is increased and creative talents are enhanced. Time to release all you carry which no longer serves your greater good. Change is eminent and the fewer burdens you carry, the easier transition for you. Face your fears, forgive others, and replace your fears with unconditional love and understanding. Now is the time to commit to a higher cause to benefit others. Serving humanitarian pursuits for the greater good will bring rewards. Compassion understanding and unconditional love define your success during this cycle.

PERSONAL YEAR

Nine is the last year in the Numerology cycle and as such, is the number of completion, harvest and rebirth. Now is the time to complete what's unfinished to make room for what you want to create next year. Clean your closet and garage, get rid of anything unnecessary in your life to lighten your load. Allow for conclusions and use your intuition to dream about the future nine years. Release whatever doesn't serve you now to make room for new beginnings in the one year next year. This is also a time to reap what you have sown and relish in the harvest of all your good works. Allow the rewards from your previous eight years to flow to you. Meditate and reflect on your past years; forgive and forget. "Letting Go" is your mantra now. There is closure on every level; relationships, careers, behaviors, and lifestyles come to a close. This is a time to be of service to others and humanity as a whole. This is a transformative year and can be challenging to those who are afraid to let go. This can be a rewarding year for those who trust in the Divine in all things. Your creativity is enhanced, so make use of your artistic abilities. Compassion and forgiveness are rewarded at every turn, so resolve your differences. Your strength and courage may be challenged. Be of service and help the community and humanitarian causes.

PERSONAL MONTH

The end of a nine-month cycle. Clean out, finish up and let go of anything not serving you. Reap the benefits of your hard work from the past eight months. Make room for new beginnings next month and use your intuition to decide what you want to create next. Be creative. Serve the greater good.

MISSING NUMBER

Without an I or R in your name you have lessons to learn about compassion and tolerance. Be of service and choose some form of humanitarian work. Try to see another point of view; allow and be understanding. Study religions or philosophy and travel to gain a broader view of humanity. Don't get caught in the details, view the bigger picture. Temper your inner critic. Soften your self-judgment and judgment of others by being more understanding, compassionate and accepting.

MULTIPLE NUMBER

If you have four or more 9's in your name from letters I and R, you hold a deep understanding for all humanity. You are committed to serving and raising the vibration of humanity for the good of all. Early years may have been challenging until you were able to process your emotions. You are creatively talented and have a strong intuition. You are devoted to family and may be overly protective. Too many 9's can indicate an unstable emotional nature exhibited by intense emotions and the melodramatic.

PLANES OF EXPRESSION

Physical

Your purpose is to serve and improve humanity for the greater good. You are the quintessential humanitarian. You can be impractical and overly generous, knowing what you give out will eventually return. You are a natural actor and prefer a life of public service.

Mental

You are concerned with humanity on a Universal scale. You are broadminded and detached, able to see the grand scheme of things. Forgiveness and unconditional love and acceptance are your foundation. You generously give yourself to any humanitarian cause you deem worthy. You relate to most any personality, but it takes time to get to know you intimately. Watch you don't lose yourself in your idealistic dreams or get pulled into the melodrama.

Emotional

You are passionate, especially about issues close to your heart. You have a wide range of emotions and can fluctuate between joyful highs to sorrowful lows in a day. You are compassionate and empathetic, but can be detached and distant. Your heart sings when you realize your efforts have made a difference in the lives of others.

Intuitive

You are naturally psychic and genuinely perceptive. Your gifts of intuition are on a global scale, allowing you to intimately connect to the happenings in the world. You have healing abilities, and when directed outward they can be the catalyst for change.

NUMBER 9 SUMMARY

Humanitarian. You are here to be of service to humanity and committed to making the world a better place. You may be an actor, hair stylist, law enforcement, or manager of a multimillion-dollar foundation. You are benevolent, kind, generous, and unconditional love flows freely. The spirit of Universal Brotherhood is defined by nine and is energized with compassion. You are multi-talented and have many creative gifts which you use to serve the masses. The nine energy is the number of completion and usually means loss to make way for new beginnings. You follow the golden rule, "Do unto others…" and do not understand why everyone else doesn't naturally follow it. Compassion and forgiveness are your foundation.

A nine year is all about completion and transformation. Finish up what you began eight years ago in your one year and make room for new beginnings next year. It is a year of endings in relationships, careers, attitudes that no longer serve you. Things will leave whether you are ready or not, so it can be a challenging year of transformation. The nine vibration is synonymous with surrender. Surrender to the Divine, the Universe, and trust the process. This is also the harvest year to reap the rewards for your hard work in the last 8 years. Create space for a rebirth in your one year.

Master Numbers

Double digit numbers 11, 22, 33 and so on, represent master numbers and carry a higher vibration. These two single digits, when together, are capable of creating something greater than when they stand alone. These numbers elevate humanity and stand for the greater good. When these numbers appear in a numerology chart, there is evidence of an opportunity to raise the consciousness of humanity. If a master number appears in your core numbers, you have the higher vibration with you to assist humanity in this evolution. This is a gift from the Universe and you have a responsibility to follow this path. You have free will, however, and may opt out of living at this higher vibration. You will revert to the energy of the lower numbers: 11 becomes 2 energy, 22 becomes 4, and 33 becomes 6. My legal name, Susan equals 11, Owens equals 22, and together they equal 33.

Master Number 11

BALANCED: *Enlightened, Psychic, Spiritual Messenger, Charismatic, Inventive, Visionary, Prophetic, Inspirational, Charming*

PASSIVE: *Hypersensitive, Apathetic, Ignores Own Gifts, Cynical, Hesitant, Fearful, Nervous, High Strung*

NEGATIVE: *Fanatical, Overzealous, Uses Divine Gifts for Self, Miser, Dishonesty*

CAREERS: *Teacher, Diplomat, Mediator, Motivational Speaker, Minister*

LIFE PATH

You walk the path of the Spiritual Messenger in search of enlightenment. Honor your intuition and follow your guidance for a rewarding walk through life. Psychic abilities come naturally to you. You have the ability to uplift and inspire humanity with your spiritual wisdom. Your charismatic character attracts seekers who look to you for inspiration and spiritual truth. Embrace a strong moral code and follow the Laws of the Universe as you walk this path. You have the soul of a humanitarian and are rewarded if you devote your life to service for the benefit of humanity. This is not an egocentric or self-centered path and success is yours when you are humble, despite the possible celebrity status. Eleven, or 11/2, in your numbers represents the desire to balance the masculine and feminine energies. You are a beacon. You want to illuminate the world with harmony and peace. You are a gifted intuitive in search of higher consciousness. Your inspirational ability enables you to uplift and teach others all you learn. You are the Spiritual Messenger. When you embrace a high moral code, attract a world of abundance. You may opt out of the higher vibration of the 11 and choose to express the two energy.

DESTINY

You are an old soul here to inspire and uplift humanity. Live by Universal principles and use your insights and philosophical thoughts to inspire others. You are highly intuitive and likely psychic. You have the ability to channel higher vibrations. You are an optimistic, idealistic, and artistic person who creates harmony and balance. A charismatic and gifted teacher with many artistic talents destined to be a beacon to the world. You are a bridge between conscious and unconscious. A firm foundation and staying grounded is needed to reach the higher levels of vibration. You follow a true spiritual path when guiding others to attain their own spiritual understanding. The darker side of life is available, should you choose to live for your own personal gain. Embrace Universal Laws and do not allow your obsessions to get the best of you. You are destined to be a lightworker and serve.

SOUL

Your heart's desire is to inspire others through your own spiritual experience. You search for spiritual enlightenment and have likely lived with this quest in other lifetimes. You have wisdom beyond your years and have the desire to make the world a better place. Truth and beauty are your visions and you want everyone to see the world through your eyes. The desire for personal growth and transformation feeds your soul. Harmony and balance are your vehicles. Following intuition and guidance will serve you to the highest degree. Peacekeeping and creating humanitarian harmony warm your heart. You are intuitive, psychic, and have prophetic abilities. Being an inspiration to all you meet is your true heart's desire.

PERSONALITY

You are a psychic, intuitive, and have a zest for life. Your quest for enlightenment and your hyper-sensitivity enhance your spiritual gifts. Using your leadership and teaching abilities, you are an inspiration to all. You are seen as kind and open-minded with wisdom beyond your years. You may have a nervous personality and be overly sensitive. You may lack the confidence to stand up for yourself and learning to say "no" will greatly aid you in your life. Interestingly, the word "no" equals 11 and you would be wise to add it to your vocabulary. Be positive and seek higher ideals for a favorable life experience. Diplomacy and counseling are natural skills.

MATURITY

Wise beyond your years, you are an inspiration to all you meet. You are a charismatic leader here to enlighten humanity. You may find metaphysics to support your spiritual quest. You are hypersensitive to the environment, food, and other's emotions. Take care of your body, mind and spirit through a balanced lifestyle. Eleven is a higher vibration to live under and requires more care. Eleven represents a double dose of living with integrity and honoring higher ideas. The two represents surrendering to a higher power and embracing the flow of life. Teaching and speaking this wisdom of living with a higher moral code and following the Divine exemplifies the 11/2 master number.

CURRENT NAME

You are encouraged to inspire humanity. Your psychic realms expand and you have optimum levels of awareness. Your leadership, speaking, counseling, and artistic skills are heightened. Through your own life experience and inherent wisdom, you are an inspiration to all.

BIRTHDAY 11, 29

You are a spiritual being, creative and brilliant. You have the ability for deep understanding being born on an 11 day. Trust in yourself and share your insights with others. You are a teacher, counselor, and are here to inspire others. You are capable of a higher level of consciousness and insight. Maintain harmony and an honorable integrity for a successful life.

MAJOR CYCLE

Formative

If you are born in November, eleven is your first major life cycle. This is a cycle of spiritual and personal growth when you have the opportunity to understand higher ideals. It is a cycle of illumination and inspiration, self-improvement and understanding Universal Laws. You are here to inspire and help others. Committing to your own personal improvement is the best way to serve humanity. You are a Spiritual Messenger and must find harmony within to become a successful leader. If the eleven vibration is too demanding, you may choose to live the two vibration of harmony, cooperation and relationship.

Progressive

If your birthday is on 11 or 29, your second major life cycle is under the eleven vibration. This Progressive cycle carries the two energy cooperation and relationship. You are a natural counselor, negotiator and teacher with a gift for public speaking. Investigating metaphysics enhances your abilities for personal growth and serving the greater good. Your own self-improvement is the foundation for this cycle and transformation and a higher spiritual understanding are your rewards.

Wisdom

The eleven energy rules now and your senior years offer you an opportunity for self-mastery and profound transformation. You are a Spiritual Messenger and through years of personal growth work, you are able to share your wisdom with humanity. You are a gifted speaker who motivates others to improve their lives. Maintain a balanced lifestyle of harmony and healthy living to be a leader to all.

PINNACLE

The eleven brings a higher vibration in which expansive personal and spiritual growth are possible. This is a time when metaphysical and spiritual pursuits are enhanced. This is a hyper sensitive time and can be a challenge. You may be inundated with information and choices, which can be confusing. The positive side is that higher consciousness and the upper realms are available to you. Connecting with the Divine Source is paramount and will guide you through this time of phenomenal spiritual advancement. Remaining balanced and grounded is key as changes can occur quickly. Adapting higher ideals enhances your probability of success. Fame is possible.

ESSENCE

You are a Lightworker, a Spiritual Messenger. You are here to uplift and inspire humanity. Eleven essence is open elevated levels of consciousness and higher spiritual energies. Humanitarian service is required of you now. Use your intuition and creativity for the study of the Divine and true self-mastery. This is a time to go inward, so spend it meditating in nature to maintain a positive attitude.

PERSONAL YEAR

The eleven year includes the aspects of the two year, but is a higher spiritual vibration. Trust your intuition, face the unknown and reach new heights. Spiritual growth, expanded consciousness, and personal transformation are all available to you this year. A positive moral code gives you a solid foundation on which to serve the greater good. Eliminate your fears and self-doubt so you do what you're put here to do, inspire and uplift humanity.

NUMBER 11 SUMMARY

You are the Spiritual Messenger. Master Numbers are the same energy as their reduced digit counterparts, but with a higher spiritual vibration. You are here to learn about consciousness and the higher realms. Your search is for enlightenment and your mission is to share with humanity all you learn. You are the inspirational teachers of the world here to uplift and the human spirit. You are sensitive, intuitive and have psychic abilities. Your cosmic purpose is to use your Divine gifts to raise the consciousness of humanity. You have the soul of a humanitarian and destined to express from a higher consciousness.

An 11/2 year carries the two energy, however, it also carries higher vibrational energies of the master number, one. It is a year filled with enhanced intuitive abilities, spiritual experiences and enlightenment. Trust your intuition more this year than any other because you will have experiences to support your transformation and spiritual awakening. Meditate, go within, and spend time in nature. Above all, be of service to humanity and share your wisdom.

Master Number 22

BALANCED: *Integrates Spiritual Wisdom with Material World, Practical Idealist, Visionary*

PASSIVE: *Apathetic, Inflated Self Importance, Indifference, False Pride, Arrogant*

NEGATIVE: *Black Magic, Misuses Power, Demands Recondition, Crime, Ruthless*

CAREERS: *Master Builder, International CEO, Politician*

LIFE PATH

Twenty-two is a higher vibration of number four and brings with it advanced skills. You are a Master Builder and an exceptional visionary. You integrate spiritual wisdom into the physical world for humanitarian pursuits. You are a master organizer; methodical, disciplined, and diligent. The double number two doubles the dose of this higher vibration with intuition and harmony. You are a master builder here to build your legacy. You are dedicated and your focus is on the future. Your creations are on a grand scale and for a greater purpose. Your desire is to rebuild the world based on a foundation of spiritual laws for humanity and the greater good. You bring a higher wisdom into practical application. You are practical, mystical, and have an understanding of sacred geometry. You are the master of your own world here to service humanity. Your diligence and commitment coupled with your spiritual insights, provide you with an extraordinary reputation. You are an authority, and deserve the respect awarded to you. You can be controlling and arrogant, but have a sensitive, intuitive side as well. If you choose to live only for your own selfish gains, you will see limited success. Through your master ability to integrate your spiritual insights and the material world, you make the world a better place.

DESTINY

The master number 22/4 gives you the knowledge you are here to build something for the greater good. You may have a sense of urgency about completing your mission. You have the ambition to manifest your big dreams for the benefit of humanity. Your spiritual connection and application are your tools to build your legacy. You are diligent, committed, and methodical. Your spiritual insights give you the visions for your magnificent dreams. You are gifted and have the ability to build your legacy of a new foundation for humanity. The twos give you a double dose of peace and harmony as well as diplomatic skills. Do not allow your lack of self-confidence prevent you from accepting your destiny to improve the world. Watch you don't get lost in the big picture that you miss the fundamental details. You may choose to opt out of this higher vibration and instead settle for minor achievements. You have the free will to do this, but know a master number is a gift from the Divine and is not bestowed upon everyone. You were given this master number because you possess the ability to achieve greatness. Fulfill your destiny and lifelong ambition to make the world a better place. Integrate your spiritual visions with the material world to manifest your legacy.

SOUL

Your heart's desire is to make a difference; to leave a legacy which makes the world a better place. You have the ambition to manifest great change in any arena. To achieve this greatness requires total commitment because it may take you a lifetime to manifest your dreams. You possess great power and coupled with a strong spiritual side give you the ability to do whatever your heart desires. You may suffer bouts of low self-esteem and insecurity, but when you adapt to the higher vibration of 22/4, your sense of self is realigned. These are lessons to be learned in understanding your true power. Remain humble and do not let your ego rule. You would do well to remember you did not create your Divine gifts or build legacy on your own. A supportive partner who shares your vision and dreams will enhance your life journey.

PERSONALITY

You are one who is able to bring his visions into material form. You are competent, practical and always with a purpose. Serious and responsible, you always get the job done. Diligence and commitment are your foundation for achievement, but lighten up and make time for rejuvenation.

MATURITY

To achieve a 22/4 Maturity, you must have an 11/2 Destiny and 11/2 Life Path. You have grand manifestations and are the quintessential Master Builder. You have integrated higher spiritual principles and adopted Universal Laws as your inner foundation. Be of service to humanity and build your legacy for the betterment of mankind.

CURRENT NAME

Brings the desire to manifest larger dreams. Enhances your insight, intuition and ability to build on a large scale. You have the desire to leave a legacy to serve humanity.

BIRTHDAY 22

You envision building for the greater good. Your diligence and methodical approach are the foundation for you managerial expertise. You appear all business, but have a sensitive side. Life is not all hard work, you need rejuvenation time.

MAJOR CYCLE

This second or third major life cycle has boundless potential. You have the ability to manifest your dreams on a grand scale. Build your legacy for the benefit of mankind, whether it is a bricks and mortar structure or a technological advancement. With your visions at a peak, bring them into the physical world. Integrity, responsibility and maintaining balance are prominent now. This is a challenging cycle with a lot at stake. You have the potential to reach a high level of self-mastery during this era. This is your achievement and reward cycle.

PINNACLE

Twenty-two energy includes all of the number four vibrations but with a higher purpose. This is your year to accomplish your grand visions and build your legacy all in service to humanity. Adapt a healthy moral code and strong work ethic to see your dreams to fruition. Stay centered and balanced to take advantage of the multitude of opportunities offered this year. Achievement and reward are yours if you keep your head, use your knowledge and persevere.

ESSENCE

Your essence refers to the inner you, so you are building with an inward focus now. New levels of consciousness and understanding are available to you now and for the future. This is your time to use this energy to serve the greater good and uplift humanity. Success and reward are yours if you have the courage and faith to learn everything available to you.

PERSONAL YEAR

This temporary cycle signifies you have the opportunity to serve humanity on a grand scale. Your heightened personal power is evident now and is accessible to you. Your intuitive skills are enhanced to empower your elevated work ethic. Now is the time to build your legacy. Use your heightened visionary skills and diligent work ethic to manifest your big dreams. Your managerial abilities are at a peak and your spiritual insights are heightened. You will learn new skills to achieve whatever you desire. Now is the time to implement your master plans. This is a challenging pinnacle because the enhanced energy is infused in every aspect of your life. With great achievements come great challenges. Have the courage and strength to face your problems and persevere. This is a time of great potential and enormous achievement. You have the opportunity to reflect back on this time of your life with great honor and satisfaction of a job well done. Perseverance, commitment and a balanced lifestyle will help you learn the lessons of this pinnacle. Use your unlimited imagination to build your legacy for the greater good.

NUMBER 22 SUMMARY

Master Builder. Master Numbers are the same energy as their reduced digit counterparts, but with a higher spiritual vibration. You have major organizational skills and a legacy to build. You are a visionary; inventive and a forward thinking creator who turns visions into reality. Your mission is to service humanity by bringing your visions into the physical world. The higher vibration of 22 gifts you with a higher awareness and abilities to serve the greater good.

A 22/4 year is one filled with aspirations and accomplishments. Focus on humanitarian efforts and making the world a better place. There is the potential for elevated personal growth this year because of the 22 higher vibration supporting you. A year for greater visions which lead to greater achievements. Be dedicated, persevere and work for the greater good for an exceptionally successful year.

Master Number 33

BALANCED: *Spiritual Advisor, Healer, Teacher, Brings Earth Mother, Cosmic Parent, Service to Humanity*

PASSIVE: *Martyr, Codependent, Rebellious, Irresponsible*

NEGATIVE: *Judgmental, Uses Gifts for Personal Gains, Narcissistic*

CAREERS: *Healer, Counselor, Teacher, Medical Intuitive*

The characteristics of number three are: Healer, Counselor, Universal Guardian, Intuitive Healer, Unconditional Love. May be rebellious, overprotective, and worries at every turn. Fears intimacy and lacks boundaries. Martyrdom. Codependency.

Thirty-three is a higher vibration of the number six and unites the Universal Spiritual Truths and the earthly plane. A sensitive visionary who serves the masses. Compassionate, empathetic, and with a nurturing heart heals humanity through selfless service. A full understanding of balance between one's own needs and those of others. Three is the number of emotional communication and the energy is doubled here. Six is the caregiver, taking on the responsibility for others. Those in need are the beneficiaries of someone with a 33/6 in their chart. A humble servant of humanity here to express loving kindness. A Universal Earth Mother.

LIFE PATH

You are a joyfully compassionate intuitive here to uplift and heal humanity. This highly spiritual vibration signifies multiple Divine blessings. You are to bring a higher consciousness of love to humanity. You are a loving caregiver with legendary skills whether administered on the young or old. Unconditional love is your driving force, not material gain or fame. You genuinely see the good in people and have an intolerance of injustice. Follow Universal Laws to bring a higher spiritual vibration to humanity. Do not get caught up in humanity's struggles, lest you scatter your energy. Stay detached and allow all your love to flow from you. This is the heart of 33/6 healing vibration. Don't aimlessly follow a path or be overly concerned with pleasing everyone. We all have our own path and life lessons to learn, retain some energy for your own path.

DESTINY

Your purpose is to joyfully serve humanity with an unconditionally loving heart. You are blessed with Divine Love and have the responsibility to share it with the world. The three energy is delightfully creative and when coupled with your drive to be of service is fulfilling your destiny. You embody compassion and are destined to unconditionally love and serve humanity. Use your creative gifts to serve and uplift the masses. You have a mission and a high purpose to bring joy to the masses. This is an unusual master number and now bestowed upon just anyone. Use these gifts from the Divine to benefit the greater good.

SOUL

Your heart's desire is to uplift humanity through joyful, loving service. You want to elevate humanitarian consciousness to embody unconditional love. 33/6 is unique and requires a commitment to a life of loving service. Caring for others brings you great joy and you have master skills.

PERSONALITY

You have excellent teaching and counseling skills built on a compassionate foundation. You focus on others' needs before yourself and have a strong moral code. You have an intolerance for injustice and strive to right wrongs. Remain detached however, do not get caught up in daily drama and reserve some energy for yourself. Put on your own oxygen mask first.

MATURITY

You must have an 11/2 or 22/4 Life Path or Destiny to achieve a 33/6 Maturity number. This is a highly spiritual gift. You are an unconditionally loving soul who radiates joy and love. Through years of loving service to humanity, you are a master healer. The Universal Laws and life experience guide you to a higher consciousness and understanding. This may be challenging at times, but trust in the Divine Order and know there is a purpose for everything. Being responsible for yourself and not the entire universe is a major life lesson. Balance the energy you give to others and reserve the same for yourself.

CURRENT NAME

33/6 energy in your name elevates your ability to uplift others. A life of service to humanity has many rewards. Teaching, counseling, caregiving skills are enhanced as are many creative abilities.

PINNACLE

Follows 11/2 and 22/4 pinnacles. The energy of a 33/6 invites the opportunity for a highly elevated change in consciousness. A time when you are able to serve humanity on a grand scale. Great achievements are possible during this challenging time. Perseverance and commitment are needed to pass the tests and learn from life's lessons. Selfless service and sacrifice are required to gain new wisdom and elevate your consciousness. Unconditional love with responsibility and detachment is the foundation to uplift humanity. Remaining grounded and balanced will allow you to soar to great heights.

ESSENCE

This master cycle essence enhances and expands your ability to love and heal. The potential to achieve great heights is open now and endless energy is required of you.

Unconditional love and compassion with selfless service are required to master this essence. This is your time to serve humanity and raise the consciousness of love in the world.

NUMBER 33 SUMMARY

Cosmic Caregiver/Healer. Master Numbers are the same energy as their reduced digit counterparts, but with a higher spiritual vibration. You have angelic connections which give you powerful healing energy. You are here to heal the masses as a medical intuitive and to create harmony wherever you are. Altruism is your foundation to share unconditional love and bring highly spiritual energy to the physical world. You are a healer through and through and as such; you surrender your life to being of service to humanity.

A 33/6 year brings in unconditional love and healing energy. Compassion and selfless service is required to bring healing and harmony to humanity. This is an incredible opportunity and huge responsibility not bestowed on just anyone. Accept the blessings from above and allow unconditional love and healing energy flow through you to others.

Karmic Debt Numbers

Karmic debt numbers appear as 13/4, 14/5, 16/7, 19/1 and signify a past lifetime of abuse. These are now lessons required to be mastered in this lifetime. They are most influential when they appear in the core numbers: Life Path, Destiny, Soul, Personality, Maturity or Birthdate. The misuse of the number represents selfishness in the past and failing to learn the lesson of the number. The number one signifies the self in each number. Number three, implies creativity talents were wasted and words were used to inflict pain. The number four in a karmic debt signifies rebelliousness and irresponsibility were used to escape diligence and structure; the misuse of freedom and liberty. The number six represents relationship and responsibility so, love and commitment were rejected for your own personal pleasure. The number nine represents spiritual wisdom and in a karmic debt, signifies this ability was for your own selfish gain at the expense of others.

13/4 DISCIPLINE

When number four appears anywhere, it means diligence is required to accomplish a goal. 13/4 is no different. This karmic debt number brings about reform and death to the existing order of things. Obstacles and setbacks are common in a lifetime with a 13/4 in their core numbers. Procrastination, laziness, and negativity are prevalent and prevent achievements and progress forward. It is a lesson of diligence, responsibility, integrity, and commitment to success. A direct approach to multiple obstacles is the way to face the challenges. Shortcuts are not an alternative to mastering this lesson. Don't scatter your energies or take the easy way out, which are options, but will not help you learn the lesson of 13/4. Focus, determination and structure are needed here. In the Tarot wisdom tradition, the number thirteen is the Death card. This signifies things will change dramatically and you are required to build a new foundation (four energy) for the future. New job, home, relationship—whatever is outdated and no longer necessary in your life will end. Authenticity, perseverance and adherence to solid moral code help release this karmic debt.

14/5 TEMPERANCE

This karmic debt brings a rebellious transformation. In an unconventional manner, life will transform. There is constant change and unexpected events which require you to adapt. Resist the many temptations (addictions) in your life and take responsibility for your actions. Moderation and balance in all aspects of your life are necessary to overcome this karmic debt. A misuse of freedom in the past requires a life of temperance and adaptability. In the Tarot tradition, fourteen is the Temperance card. You will need moderation to work through this karmic debt. Have a strong moral code and commit to following it in this lifetime. Don't fall victim to failure and escape into addiction. Believe in yourself and don't give up. Choose the middle path to find balance and build a stable foundation to enable clarity and concentration. Being grounded will allow the freedom to be adaptable and go with the ever changing flow of life.

16/7 AWAKENING

This karmic debt signifies sudden drastic change in a lifetime for the purpose of awakening the spirit. Previous love affairs, taking advantage of loved ones for your own gain is the basis for this karmic debt. This is the opportunity for destruction to rebuild and transform your life. In the Tarot's numerology sixteen, this is the Tower card which signifies everything not on a firm foundation will crumble. It is the devastation of the old and rebuilding anew. Truths are revealed, deep emotions are heightened, all for the purpose of spiritual awareness. In the past, your ego was in control and the result now is a struggle between it and a higher power. A seven requires inner reflection and the ability to bring spiritual principles to the material world. Allow Universal

Guidance to direct you to a new awakening and rebirth. Be authentic and respect those you love to release the debt.

16/7 ESSENCE

The 16/7 energy is a clearing away of anything unnecessary for your future. This is a dark night of the soul cycle when you can go deep into yourself and have a spiritual cleansing. You can expect the unexpected and there can be many tumultuous events during this year. Surrender is the key to survival because ultimately, you will emerge a better human being. There are Divine forces in control so trust them to guide you through this turbulent time. There is much to learn now and be open to the great lessons in front of you. Feel gratitude for what you have rather than lament what you don't possess. Continually look at the lighter side of life instead of focusing on the glass half empty. You will have a greater understanding and see from higher levels of consciousness.

19/1 ABUSE OF POWER

The opportunity to face a life challenge all on your own defines this karmic debt. The wisdom of numbers one and nine are required to overcome the obstacle and learn from the experience. You will have many opportunities to defend yourself on your own. You will learn to stand up for yourself by yourself. Asking for help and accepting advice from others are the foundation of this karmic debt. Spiritual power for selfish gain and self-fulfillment created this debt; compassion and understanding for humanity will release it. The lesson to learn here is you are not alone; we are all connected. 19/1 karmic debt requires surrender to the Divine and devotion to serving humanity for the greater good.

19/1 ESSENCE

This is an independent era; a time when you are striving for independence and setting yourself apart. This is a challenging essence and you may find yourself struggling to balance your personal ambitions with serving the greater good. Now is the time to integrate your outer worldly desires with your inner spiritual self. You may need more solitude for inner reflection and yet feel the world pulling you outward. Your achievements are substantial, but you may have fewer relationships within your circle.

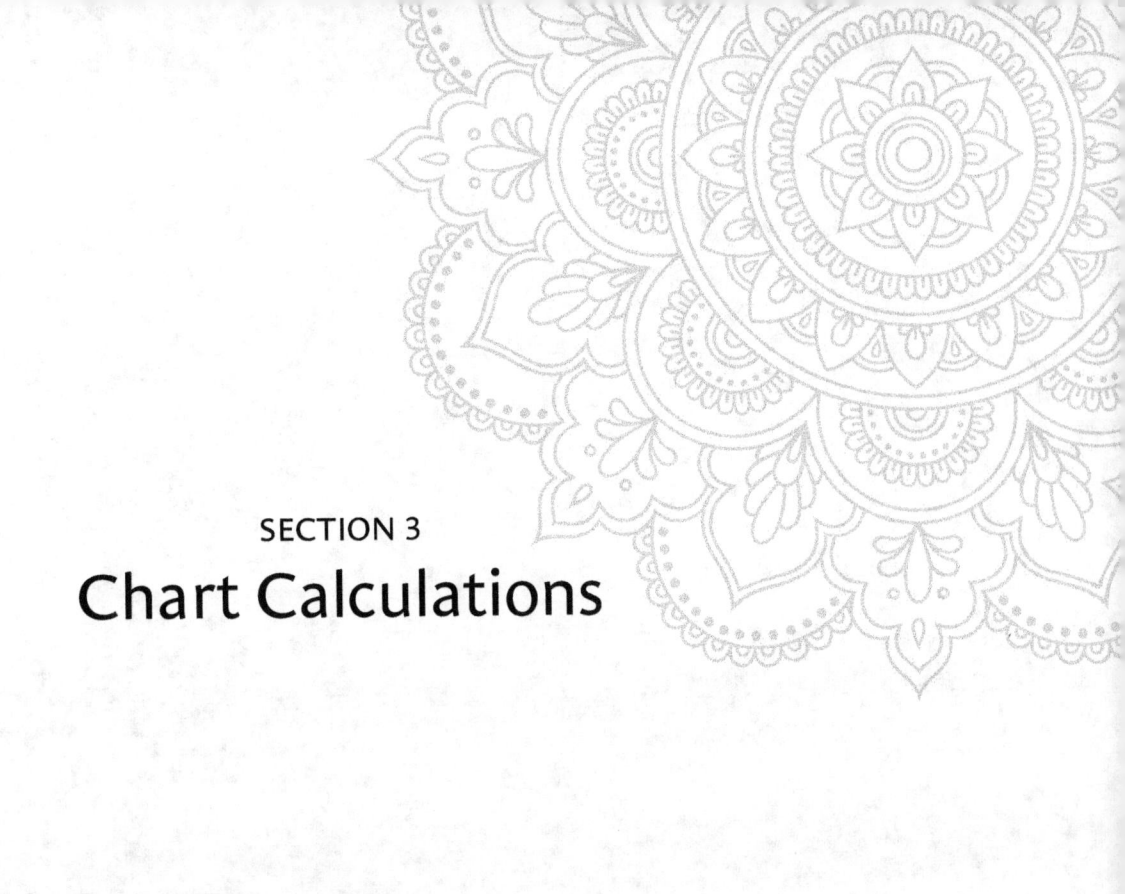

SECTION 3

Chart Calculations

Chart Calculations

In this section, you will find all the calculations needed to complete a Numerology Chart. Life Path, Major Cycles, Pinnacles, Challenges, and Personal Year are all created from your birthday. The name on your birth certificate creates your Destiny, Soul, Personality, Maturity, Planes of Expression, as well as the Essence Number and Transit Chart. For the purpose of explanation, I have created Sophia Chloe Madison, born May 11, 1990 as an example to illustrate how to create your own Numerology Chart. In the first half of this segment you use your birthday. In the second half, you will use the name on your birth certificate.

If, after visiting with the calculations you find that you want assistance, you can do one or both of the following. First you can contact me through my website (information is at the back of the book) and we can do a reading together. Second, there are online resources for creating a chart and links to those can be found on my website also. I will keep them updated with the best options.

Birthday Calculations

Sophia Chloe Madison — May 11, 1990

LIFE PATH

To calculate your Life Path, reduce all numbers in your birthday to single digits except Master Numbers (11, 22, 33).

Example: May 11, 1990

Step 1

5-11-1990 becomes: 5 + 11 + 1*

*Calculate the year by reducing down:
$$1990 = 1 + 9 + 9 + 0 = 19, 1 + 9 = 10, 1 + 0 = 1$$
$$1990 = 19 = 10 = 1$$

Step 2

Add the numbers across for your Life Path number: 5+1+1+1 = 8

Sophia's Life Path is 8.

WATCH FOR MASTER NUMBERS: 11, 22, 33

Sophia has a Master Number for her birthday, 11. Master Numbers represent a higher vibration of the reduced number. 11/2, 22/4, 33/6. They carry a spiritual influence and indicate a time of greater understanding of a higher level of consciousness.

MAJOR CYCLES

There are three Major Cycles in a lifetime that run consecutively.

- The first is the *Formative* cycle and runs 24-30 years and carries the energy of your birth month.
- The second Major Cycle is the *Progressive* cycle and runs about 27 years and is ruled by the day of your birth.
- The third Major Cycle is the *Wisdom* cycle and runs throughout the rest of your life.

This last cycle carries the energy of your birth year.

To determine your own Major Cycle schedule, calculate your Life Path and refer to the chart on the following page. Major Cycles always begin in a one year, so check the chart for the age in which your one year begins closest to the ages below. The birthdate rules the cycles.

For Sophia's 5-11-1990 birthday, her Life Path is 8.

- Her Formative cycle begins at age 0 to about 28 years and carries the 5 energy from the month of May.
- Her Progressive cycle begins at approximately age 29 and runs until about age 56. This cycle carries 11/2 energy from her day of birth.
- Her Wisdom cycle begins about age 57 for the rest of her life and has 1 energy from her birth year.

CHART OF MAJOR CYCLES

Life Path	Formative Cycle	Progressive Cycle Begins	Wisdom Cycle Begins
1	Age 0	27 Years	54 Years
2/11	Age 0	26 Years	53 Years
3	Age 0	34 Years	61 Years
4/22	Age 0	33 Years	60 Years
5	Age 0	32 Years	59 Years
6/33	Age 0	31 Years	58 Years
7	Age 0	30 Years	57 Years
8	Age 0	29 Years	56 Years
9	Age 0	28 Years	55 Years

PINNACLES

There are four pinnacles in a lifetime and run concurrently with Master Cycles. These four phases of life indicate the conditions and opportunities present in each pinnacle. Every pinnacle reveals possible achievements and areas of focus to assist you when facing your challenge. When you master the pinnacle, you have greater potential for success in facing the obstacles presented in the challenge.

- The *first pinnacle* represents self-discovery and self-actualization.
- The *second pinnacle* reveals your relationship with others.
- The *third pinnacle* represents maturity.
- The *fourth* is self mastery.

1. To calculate the first pinnacle, add the birth month and the birthday together.
2. The second pinnacle is calculated by adding the birthday and the birth year together.
3. To calculate the third pinnacle, add the two previous sums together.
4. To calculate the fourth pinnacle, add the birth month and birth year together.

- Reduce all numbers before adding.
- The first pinnacle ends the same year as the Formative cycle.
- The second and third pinnacles last nine years.
- The fourth pinnacle begins at the end of the third pinnacle and lasts throughout the rest of your lifetime.

To calculate the Pinnacles, follow this chart and example:

For a birthdate of May 11, 1990: 5-11-1   Reduced becomes: 5-2-1

First Pinnacle	Add	Birth Month	+	Birth Day	$5+2 = 7$
Second Pinnacle	Add	Birthday	+	Birth Year	$2+1 = 3$
Third Pinnacle	Add	First Pinnacle	+	Second Pinnacle	$7+3 = 1$
Fourth Pinnacle	Add	Birth Month	+	Birth Year	$5+1 = 6$

CHALLENGES

The four challenge numbers are on the same timeline as pinnacle numbers and run concurrently with Master Cycles. Challenges are obstacles to be overcome; lessons to be learned for you to reach your full potential. Courageously face the challenge to reap the rewards of the pinnacle. Challenge numbers cannot be ignored. Lessons will continue to appear until they are mastered.

1. To calculate the first challenge, subtract the birth month from the birthday.
2. The second challenge is calculated by subtracting the birthday from the birth year.
3. To calculate the third challenge, subtract the two previous sums.
4. To calculate the fourth challenge, subtract the birth month from the birth year.

- Reduce all days before subtracting.
- The first challenge ends the same year as the formative cycle.
- The second and third challenges last nine years.
- The fourth challenge begins at the end of the third challenge and lasts throughout the rest of your lifetime.
- The third challenge may have an influence throughout a lifetime.
- The fourth challenge is the most demanding.

To calculate the Challenges, follow this chart and example:

For a birthdate of May 11, 1990: 5-11-1   Reduced becomes: 5-2-1

First Challenge	Subtract Birth Month	-	Birth Day	5 - 2 = 3
Second Challenge	Subtract Birth Day	-	Birth Year	2 - 1 = 1
Third Challenge	Subtract First Challenge	-	Second Challenge	3 - 1 = 2
Fourth Challenge	Subtract Birth Month	-	Birth Year	5 - 1 = 4

PERSONAL YEAR

Numerology functions on a nine year cycle and changes every January. To calculate the universal year, add the numbers in the year. 2023 = 2 + 2 + 3 = 7 for a universal year of 7.

Your personal year changes every January as well but, to make it personal, add only your birth month and your day of birth to the current universal year. Disregard your birth year for this calculation. For example:

Birth Month + Birth Day + Current Year = Personal Year

May 11 birthday in the year 2023 = 5 + 11 (reduces to 5 + 2) + 7 = 14   1 + 4 = 5   **5 Personal Year in 2023**

If you have an understanding of your personal year's energy, you know how to live in harmony with that vibration and have a more harmonious and productive year.

1 A **one** year is focused outward as you plant seeds for what you want to accomplish in the next nine years.

2 A **two** year is an inward focus, when you nurture your seeds and is slower than the previous year.

3 A **three** year is a blending of the previous years and a time when creativity flows. It is a social year and fast-paced and outwardly focused time.

4 A **four** year is a year to set up a new foundation with your nose to the grindstone. You'll work hard this year and create a structure stable enough to see you through the changing five year.

5 The outwardly focused **five** year is all about freedom and expansion. This is your year to grow and you'll need the grounding of the four year for stability during this highly volatile time.

6 The **six** year is home and family and a time to integrate all your one-five years. Relationship and responsibility is the focus in this inward year.

7 The spiritual **seven** year is a time for inner reflection and self improvement. Ask life's big questions and do your research. Go on a vision quest.

8 The **eight** year is a time to direct your management and organizational skills to your life. This is an outward year when money flows in greater frequency.

9 The inner reflective **nine** year is time endings and rebirths. Let go of what is no longer needed to make space for the new seeds planted next year.

IN SUMMARY

1	New Beginnings, Action
2	Cooperation, Balance
3	Communication, Expression
4	Building, Planning
5	Movement, Change
6	Responsibility, Universal Love
7	Introspection, Personal Growth
8	Karmic Justice, Power
9	Endings, Completions
11/2	Illumination, Higher Learning
22/4	Accomplishment, Transformation
33/6	Universal Healer, Nurturer

Birth Certificate Calculations

To calculate your Destiny, Soul, Personality, Maturity, Essence, and Planes of Expression, use the name on your birth certificate. This is who you came into being and is the most accurate name to use when forming your Numerology chart. Repeat the process for your Destiny, Soul and Personality numbers using your current name and the same method of calculation. If it is the same name on your birth certificate, you double the energy of those numbers.

Below are letters with their numerical value. Write out your name and place the numerical value next to each letter in your name. Put the number for the vowels **above** your name for the Soul number and place the numbers for the consonants **below** your name for the Personality number. This is important to keep the numbers separate for calculations. I use Sophia Chloe Madison as an example.

1 = A, J, S
2 = B, K, T
3 = C, L, U
4 = D, M, V
5 = E, N, W
6 = F, O, X
7 = G, P, Y
8 = H, Q, Z
9 = I, R

6 9 1		6 5	1 9 6	= 6 + 9 + 1 + 6 + 5 + 1 + 9 + 6 = 43 4 + 3 = 7
S O P H I A	C H L O E		M A D I S O N	
1 7 8	3 8 3		4 4 1 5	= 1 + 7 + 8 + 3 + 8 + 3 + 4 + 4 +1 + 5 = 44/8 4 + 4 = 8

SOUL NUMBER
Write the numerical value of the vowel above your Birth Certificate name.

6   9 1 $6 + 9 + 1 = 16$ $1 + 6 = \mathbf{7}$

S O P H I A

6 5 $6 + 5 = \mathbf{11}$

C H L O E

1   9   6 $1 + 9 + 6 = 16$ $1 + 6 = \mathbf{7}$

M A D I S O N

$7 + 11 + 7 = 25$ $2 + 5 = 7$ Soul Number 7

PERSONALITY NUMBER
Write the numerical value of the consonant below your Birth Certificate name.

S O P H I A

1   7 8 $1 + 7 + 8 = 16$ $1 + 6 = \mathbf{7}$

C H L O E

3 8 3 $3 + 8 + 3 = 14$ $1 + 4 = \mathbf{5}$

M A D I S O N

4   4   1   5 $4 + 4 +1 + 5 = 14$ $1 + 4 = \mathbf{5}$

$7 + 5 + 5 = 17$ $1 + 7 = 8$ Personality Number 8

DESTINY NUMBER

To calculate your Destiny, add your Soul and Personality Numbers together.

$7 + 8 = 15$ $1 + 5 = 6$ **Destiny 6**

MATURITY NUMBER

To calculate your Maturity Number, add your Life Path and Destiny numbers together.

Life Path 8   Destiny 6 $8 + 6 = 14/5$ **Maturity 5**

This is a Karmic Debt number. Sophia's Maturity number is 5, but because it is 14/5 carries Karmic Debt qualities. (see Karmic Debt Numbers)

CURRENT NAME

6		9	5		1	9		6		$= 6 + 9 + 5 = 20$	$1 + 9 + 6 = 16$	$20 + 16 = 36$	$3 + 6 = $ **9**
S	O	P	H	I	A	M	A	D	I	S	O	N	
1		7	8			4		4	1		5		$= 1 + 7 + 8 = 16$ $4 + 4 + 1 + 5 = 14$ $16 + 14 = 30 = $ **3**

Current Name Soul Number 9
Current Name Personality Number 3
Current Name Destiny Number 3 $(9 + 3 = 12$ $1 + 2 = 3)$

Planes of Expression

Our physical selves rely on our senses to experience life. Our mental selves depend on our intellectual brain whereas our emotional selves are based on our feelings. Our intuitive selves access the higher realms and are based on our perceptions. This is the way you behave, think, feel, and sense life. After your calculations, see which number is the highest: physical, mental, emotional or spiritual. The highest number reflects which ability you use more. These numbers represent how you handle life's problems.

To calculate your Planes of Expression, refer to the numbers in your birth certificate name. Count the number of times each number appears in your name. 4's and 5's represent your physical self. 1's and 8's represent your mental self. 2's, 3's, and 6's are your emotional self. 7's and 9's are your intuitive self. Then separate the numbers into these categories:

Physical: 4, 5
Mental: 1, 8
Emotional: 2, 3, 6
Intuitive: 7, 9

The numerical value of vowels is written above the name and the value of the consonants below the name for easier diagnosis. Add the total number of letters in your name to double check the totals.

6		9	1				6	5		1		9		6	(8 letters)
S	O	P	H	I	A		C	H	L	O	E		M	A	D	I	S	O	N	(18 letters)
1		7	8				3	8	3				4		4		1		5	(10 letters)

Total of each number

1's	4
2's	0
3's	2
4's	1
5's	2
6's	4
7's	1
8's	2
9's	2
	18 total letters

Physical	(4, 5)	= 3
Mental	(1, 8)	= 6
Emotional	(2, 3, 6)	= 6
Intuitive	(7, 9)	= 3
		= 18 total letters

Transit Chart

This calculation is complicated and requires a considerable amount of time and concentration to complete accurately. If this segment is too challenging, you may order a complete numerology chart from my website: wisdomofnumerology.com.

Age
Year
First Name (Physical)
Middle Name (Mental)
Last Name (Spiritual)
Essence Number
Personal Year
Major Cycle
Pinnacle
Challenge

1: A J S   2: B K T   3: C L U   4: D M V   5: E N W   6: F O X   7: G P Y   8: H Q Z   9: I R

TRANSIT CHART

Age	0	1	2	3	4	5	6	7	8	9	10	11	12	13	14	15	16	17	18	19	20	21	22	23	24
Year																									
First																									
Middle																									
Last																									
Essence																									
Personal Year																									
Major Cycle																									
Pinnacle																									
Challenge																									

AGE

This number is on the chart as 0 for your first year.

YEAR

Write the year of your birth in the box below Age 0 and continue the sequence throughout the chart. The year and your age give you a reference point for your timeline.

TRANSIT LETTERS

This is your name written in the chart with their numerical values. On this transit segment, your name is divided by first, middle and last. Your first name is your physical self, your middle name is your mental self and your last name is your spiritual self. The letter determines how many times it repeats in your chart. For instance, a S has a value of 1, therefore it repeats once in the sequence. The letter O has a value of 4, therefore it repeats four times in the sequence. The value of P is 7 and therefore repeats seven times in the sequence, and so on. For the name Sophia Chloe Madison, the sequence would appear like this:

SOPHIA: S-1, O-6, P-7, H-8, I-9, A-1
S OOOOOO PPPPPPP HHHHHHHH IIIIIIIII A

CHLOE: C-3, H-8, L-3, O-6, E-5
CCC HHHHHHHH LLL OOOOOO EEEEE

MADISON appears like this: M-4, A-1, D-4, I-9, S-1, O-6, N-5
MMMM A DDDD IIIIIIIII S OOOOOO NNNNN

Repeat this sequence throughout the chart to 99 years.

1: A J S   2: B K T   3: C L U   4: D M V   5: E N W   6: F O X   7: G P Y   8: H Q Z   9: I R

Age	0	1	2	3	4	5	6	7	8	9	10	11	12	13	14	15	16	17	18	19	20	21	22	23	24
Year	90	91	92	93	94	95	96	97	98	99	0	1	2	3	4	5	6	7	8	9	10	11	12	13	14
First	S-1	O-6	O-6	O-6	O-6	O-6	O-6	P-7	P-7	P-7	P-7	P-7	P-7	P-7	H-8	H-8	H-8	H-8	H-8	H-8	H-8	H-8	I-9	I-9	I-9
Middle	C-3	C-3	C-3	H-8	H-8	H-8	H-8	H-8	H-8	H-8	H-8	L-3	L-3	L-3	O-6	O-6	O-6	O-6	O-6	O-6	E-5	E-5	E-5	E-5	E-5
Last	M-4	M-4	M-4	M-4	A-1	D-4	D-4	D-4	D-4	I-9	I-9	I-9	I-9	I-9	I-9	I-9	I-9	I-9	S-1	O-6	O-6	O-6	O-6	O-6	O-6
Essence	8	13	13	18	15	18	18	19	19	24	24	19	19	19	23	23	23	23	15	20	19	19	20	20	20
Personal Year	8	9	1	2	3	4	5	6	7	8	9	1	2	3	4	5	6	7	8	9	1	2	3	4	5
Major Cycle	5	5	5	5	5	5	5	5	5	5	5	5	5	5	5	5	5	5	5	5	5	5	5	5	5
Pinnacle	7	7	7	7	7	7	7	7	7	7	7	7	7	7	7	7	7	7	7	7	7	7	7	7	7
Challenge	4	4	4	4	4	4	4	4	4	4	4	4	4	4	4	4	4	4	4	4	4	4	4	4	4

ESSENCE

The Essence number is the total value of your first, middle and last names. In year 0, the letters are S, C and M. Add the numerical values of these three numbers to get the Essence number. The value of S is 1. The value of C is 3 and the value of M is 4.

For example: S + C + M = 8   1 + 3 + 4 = 8 Essence

Write the year of your birth in the box below Age 0 and continue the sequence throughout the chart. The Essence number presents the inner you and your inner world, whereas the Personal Year number describes your outer world.

PERSONAL YEAR

On the Transit Chart, your first personal year is the same as your Life Path number (add the month, day, and year of your birth together). Once that number is entered into the personal year, numbers 1-9 are repeated. For instance, in Sophia's chart, her birthday is May 11, 1990. Her first personal year is an 8 (5 + 2 + 1 = 8) and an 8 is put under Age 0. Under age 1, write a 9 and because numerology cycles through 1-9, under age 2, the cycle begins again with 1. Age 3 = 2 personal year, 4 = 3 personal year and so on.

SOPHIA CHLOE MADISON'S NUMEROLOGY CHART

Life Path	8
Destiny	6
Soul	7
Personality	8
Maturity	14/5
Current Name	3
Day of Birth	11/2
Planes of Expression	
Physical	3
Mental	6
Emotional	6
Intuitive	3

My Numerology Chart

Enter your personal numerology in the table below. Use the blank charts on the following pages to calculate your numerology from age 0-99 and determine your Personal Year and Essence Transits. When you understand each year's numerical energy, you can choose how to live in harmony with that vibration to create a more balanced and rewarding year.

MY NUMEROLOGY CHART

Life Path   _____

Destiny   _____

Soul   _____

Personality   _____

Maturity   _____

Current Name   _____

Day of Birth   _____

Planes of Expression

      Physical   _____

      Mental   _____

      Emotional   _____

      Intuitive   _____

Wisdom of Numerology

1: A J S   2: B K T   3: C L U   4: D M V   5: E N W   6: F O X   7: G P Y   8: H Q Z   9: I R

Age	0	1	2	3	4	5	6	7	8	9	10	11	12	13	14	15	16	17	18	19	20	21	22	23	24
Year																									
First																									
Middle																									
Last																									
Essence																									
Personal Year																									
Major Cycle																									
Pinnacle																									
Challenge																									

1: A J S   2: B K T   3: C L U   4: D M V   5: E N W   6: F O X   7: G P Y   8: H Q Z   9: I R

Age	25	26	27	28	29	30	31	32	33	34	35	36	37	38	39	40	41	42	43	44	45	46	47	48	49
Year																									
First																									
Middle																									
Last																									
Essence																									
Personal Year																									
Major Cycle																									
Pinnacle																									
Challenge																									

1: A J S   2: B K T   3: C L U   4: D M V   5: E N W   6: F O X   7: G P Y   8: H Q Z   9: I R

Age	50	51	52	53	54	55	56	57	58	59	60	61	62	63	64	65	66	67	68	69	70	71	72	73	74
Year																									
First																									
Middle																									
Last																									
Essence																									
Personal Year																									
Major Cycle																									
Pinnacle																									
Challenge																									

1: A J S   2: B K T   3: C L U   4: D M V   5: E N W   6: F O X   7: G P Y   8: H Q Z   9: I R

Age	75	76	77	78	79	80	81	82	83	84	85	86	87	88	89	90	91	92	93	94	95	96	97	98	99
Year																									
First																									
Middle																									
Last																									
Essence																									
Personal Year																									
Major Cycle																									
Pinnacle																									
Challenge																									

Suzan Owens
suzan@wisdomofnumerology.com
wisdomofnumerology.com